ORIGINS

ORIGINS

REBECCA STEFOFF

Marshall Cavendish Benchmark
99 White Plains Road
Tarrytown, New York 10591
www.marshallcavendish.us

LIBRARY OF CONGRESS CATALOGING-IN-PUBLICATION DATA
Stefoff, Rebecca   Origins / by Rebecca Stefoff.   p. cm. — (Humans : an evolutionary history)
Includes bibliographical references and index.   Summary: "Describes the search for the earliest human
ancestors, from ancient apes to the australopiths"—Provided by publisher.   ISBN 978-0-7614-4183-0
1. Fossil hominids. 2. Human beings—Origin. I. Title.   GN282.S85 2010   569.9—dc22   2008034335

Editor: Joyce Stanton   Publisher: Michelle Bisson   Art Director: Anahid Hamparian
Series Designer: Meghan Dewar/MichaelNelsonDesign   Drawings, charts, and map by Robert Romagnoli

Images provided by Debbie Needleman, Picture Researcher, Portsmouth, NH from the following sources: Front
Cover: ©Kenneth Garrett/National Geographic/Getty Images. Back Cover: ©CHRIS JOHNS/National Geographic Image Collection. Pages i, 62, 72, 75: ©John Reader/Photo Researchers, Inc.; pages ii–iii: ©Michael K.
Nichols/National Geographic/Getty Images; pages vi (top), 20 (top): Portrait of Thomas Henry Huxley (1825-
95) by Alphonse Legros (1837-1911). ©Private Collection/The Bridgeman Art Library; pages vi (second from
top), 37: ©Pascal Goetgheluck/Photo Researchers, Inc.; pages vi (third from top), 45: ©Publiphoto/Photo
Researchers, Inc.; pages vi (fourth from top), 58, 69 (right), 99: ©Pat Sullivan/Associated Press; pages vi (fifth from
top, bottom), 84: ©CLIVE BROMHALL/OSF/Animals Animals; pages vii (top), 30: ©Toni Angermayer/Photo
Researchers, Inc.; pages vii (bottom), 24: Denis Farrell/Associated Press; page 8: The photograph of Prof. Dart,
forms part of the holdings of the University of the Witwatersrand, Johannesburg and is published with the kind
permission of the University of the Witwatersrand, Johannesburg; page 10: ©Philippe Plailly/Photo Researchers,
Inc.; page 13: HIP/Art Resource, NY. English Heritage, National Monuments Record, Great Britain; page 14:
HIP/Art Resource, NY; page 16: A Venerable Orang Outang, from "The Hornet" (pencil and charcoal on paper)
by English School (19th c). ©Private Collection/The Bridgeman Art Library; pages 20 (bottom), 55: ©George
Bernard/Photo Researchers, Inc.; page 25: Yoav Lemmer/Associated Press; pages 26, 82, 98: ©The Natural His-
tory Museum/The Image Works; page 35: ©Kenneth Garrett; page 38: Dr. Russell L. Ciochon/PaleoPics.com; page
42: Nature-M.P.F.T./Getty Images; page 46: ©James King-Holmes/Photo Researchers, Inc.; page 49:
©Reuters/Antony Njuguna/CORBIS; page 53: ©Science/Associated Press; page 56: ©Art Wolfe/Photo
Researchers, Inc.; page 60: SPL/Photo Researchers, Inc.; pages 64-65: ©Bettmann/CORBIS; page 69 (left): Dave
Einsel/Getty Images; page 70: ©Peter Carsten/National Geographic/Getty Images; page 74: Kenneth
Garrett/National Geographic/Getty Images; page 76: REUTERS/Euan Denholm; page 80: akg-images,
London/Hess. Landesmuseum; page 87: ©Mauricio Anton/Photo Researchers, Inc.; page 93: ©JON
JICHA/National Geographic Image Collection

Printed in Malaysia
135642

Cover: A 2-million-year-old fossil of Australopithecus robustus, discovered in South Africa
Half-title page: The footprint of a human ancestor, preserved in volcanic ash at Laetoli in Africa
Title page: A volunteer zoo worker bonds with a captive chimpanzee.
Back cover: Africa's Great Rift Valley, source of many human fossils

With special thanks

to Ian Tattersall, Curator, Division of Anthropology,

American Museum of Natural History, New York,

for his valuable comments and careful reading of the manuscript.

CONTENTS

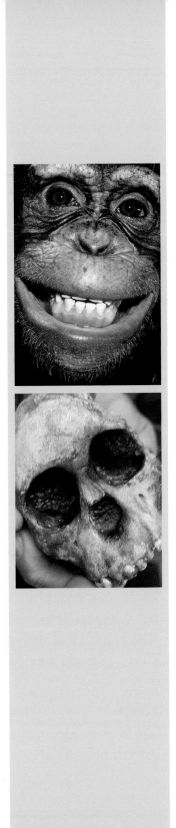

In Search of Human Origins

A young man named Raymond Dart got dressed with special care one November day in 1924. He was getting ready to serve as best man at a friend's wedding, which was going to take place at Dart's home in Johannesburg, South Africa. Dart was almost ready, just about to fasten his collar, when someone delivered several crates of broken limestone rocks to the house.

The rocks were a gift from a geologist who had recently come from a limestone quarry at a place called Taung, about a day's drive from Johannesburg. Dart

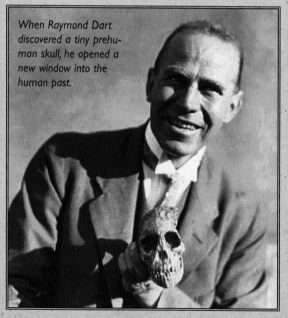

When Raymond Dart discovered a tiny prehuman skull, he opened a new window into the human past.

had heard that the geologist was going to visit the quarry, where explosives were being used to blast the limestone out of the ground. He had asked the geologist to bring him any of the newly disturbed rocks that appeared to contain fossils—ancient materials such as bones or plants that had turned to stone over time. Now the man had dropped off a load of rocks for Dart to examine.

Dart opened one of the crates, looked through its contents, and found nothing special. Still, he decided, he could spare enough time for a peek at the contents of another crate. As soon as he opened it, he forgot about the wedding.

Two Pieces of a Puzzle

Nestled among the sharp-edged chunks of rock in the crate was a small, rounded, veined lump of stone. Thanks to Dart's scientific training—he was an anatomist, a specialist in the physical structure of living things—he knew what it was. He recognized the rounded lump as an endocranial cast, a fossil that had formed inside a skull. Dart later recalled, "The convolutions and furrows of the brain and the blood vessels of the skull were plainly visible."[1] Dart had found a perfect replica of an ancient brain. But what kind of brain was it?

He thought he might be able to answer that question if he could find the skull that had once held the brain. Dart guessed that the skull had become separated from the endocranial cast during work at the quarry. It might be in one of the crates. Or it might be lost forever, blasted into powder by a dynamite charge.

Someone banged on the door of Dart's room. It was the groom, impatient for his best man to finish dressing. Guests were arriving, expecting a wedding. Dart hastily brushed the limestone dust from his trousers, put on his jacket and tie, and took his place at the groom's side. As soon as the ceremony was over, he raced back to the crate and resumed his search for the missing skull. To his delight, he found a piece of rock with a hollow that exactly matched the endocranial cast. The rock, Dart realized, contained what remained of the skull. Unfortunately, the bony remains were thickly crusted with breccia, a rocky mixture of limestone, sand, and gravel—in other words, naturally formed cement. Not until the breccia was removed from the skull would Dart know what kind of creature had possessed the brain that made the cast.

Although Dart was not a paleontologist, a specialist in the study of fossils and other relics of ancient life forms, he knew that he had to handle his find with care. If he tried knocking the breccia away from the bone with a large hammer and chisel, he might easily shatter the hollow fossil. Instead, Dart buried the rock containing the skull in a box of sand that would support and cushion it as he worked. Slowly, carefully, he tapped away on a small chisel, removing the breccia a little bit at a time. When he had worked his way close to the bone, he switched to a more delicate tool—one of his wife's knitting needles that he had sharpened to a point. He picked at the breccia with the needle until the fossil was clean.

The Taung child was a rare fossil find—not just an empty skull, but a model of the brain, with all of its folds and veins plain to see.

It took Dart seventy-three days to clean the skull, but when he was finished he held two pieces of an unusual fossil find: an ancient skull and a model of the brain that had once rested inside that skull. What kind of creature had it been?

At first, Dart had thought that he had discovered an unknown, extinct species of baboon. But by the time he had finished cleaning the skull, Dart was convinced that it had not belonged to a baboon. Instead, he believed he had found something entirely different—unlike anything scientists had ever seen before.

The skull was clearly that of a juvenile or immature individual. Like the jaw of any juvenile ape or human, the fossil jaw held a combination of milk, or childhood, teeth and adult, or permanent, teeth. Other features of the Taung skull formed a unique combination of ape and human characteristics. Surely, Dart thought, his fossil belonged somewhere on the human family tree. It must be a distant ancestor—a vital clue to the origins of humankind. But when Dart published a description of his find and his ideas about its importance, the leading scientists of the 1920s scoffed at him. A famous and respected British anatomist named Sir Arthur Keith declared that Dart's fossil had come from a deformed ape.[2]

The scientific debate over Raymond Dart's discovery, which became known as the Taung child, lasted for decades. The debate was part of humankind's search for information about its own beginnings. In time, that search would lead to an understanding of the Taung child's place in human evolution.

Darwin's Big Idea

To understand the story of human evolution, we must know something about evolution in general. Evolution is the pattern of biological change over time as new species appear and old ones die out. The basic unit of evolution is not the individual organism, or living thing. Instead, evolution occurs at the level of species, or types of living thing.

Biologists admit that *species* is a somewhat slippery term to define, and they have taken a variety of approaches to the definition. For many years, one of the most widespread definitions said that a species is a group of plants or animals that are reproductively isolated from other organisms. Reproductive isolation does not mean that the plants or animals are stranded on a desert island, lonely and unable to find mates. It means that under natural conditions the plants or animals within the species reproduce with each other but not with organisms outside the species. One problem with this definition is that it does not apply to organisms such as bacteria that can reproduce on their own, without partners.

In recent years, as researchers have decoded the genomes, or genetic signatures, of an ever-growing number of organisms, many scientists have added a genetic element to their definitions of *species*. They now call a species a group of organisms that share the same genome and, if they reproduce sexually, do so only with other organisms in the group. A species may be distributed over a wide or even a worldwide range, like modern humans, or it may occupy a range as small as a single tree, like some rain forest insects.

Since ancient times people have grouped plants and animals into species, but they thought that species were permanent and unchanging. Life on Earth, in other words, had always been the same. By the nineteenth century, however, new scientific insights were challenging that view. Geology had shown that Earth is far older than people once believed; we now know that the age of our planet is measured in billions, not thousands, of years. Naturalists, people who study the natural world, had examined fossils of dinosaurs and other creatures that no longer existed, and they realized that many kinds of life had become extinct. And if species could disappear into extinction, some naturalists asked, could they also appear? Had new species come on the scene during the long history of life?

The answer to that question came from a British naturalist named Charles Darwin. Although a number of other naturalists were exploring the question of species at around the same time, Darwin was the first to reach a wide audience. After pondering and testing his ideas for more than twenty years, in 1859 Darwin published *On the Origin of Species*, a book that he called "one long argument" in support of his central claim.[3] That claim was that species change over time, and that new species develop from existing ones. At first Darwin did not use the word "evolution" to refer to this ongoing pattern. He called it "descent with modification." The term "evolution" appeared in the fifth edition of the *Origin* in 1869, however, and ever since then it has been linked to Darwin.

Charles Darwin transformed our understanding of life with the insight that species change over time, a process known as evolution. Unhappily aware that his ideas would challenge traditional views, Darwin hesitated for years before publishing them.

New species evolved, Darwin explained, through a process that he called natural selection. He pointed out that humans have created many breeds, or varieties, of domesticated animals and plants through artificial selection, by choosing plants or animals that have desirable qualities and breeding them with each other. Artificial selection has enabled people to mold dogs, for example, into varieties that range from huge, hairy sheepdogs to tiny, bald chihuahuas. Something similar occurs in the natural world, Darwin argued. Over long periods of time, natural selection creates not just new varieties within species but distinct new species.

It works like this: Organisms pass on their characteristics to their offspring, but the characteristics inherited by the offspring include random, natural changes known as variations. If the variations help an organism's offspring—or, at least, do not harm them—then the offspring will survive to reproduce, passing on their characteristics, including the new features, to their own offspring. In time, as individuals possessing the new features reproduce with each other, those features will be reinforced as they spread through the population. At some point the organisms that evolved with the new features will be different enough from the original organisms to be considered a new species.

Natural selection explained how evolution could take place. In the struggle to survive, Darwin claimed, some organisms inherited favorable variations that gave them advantages in their particular environments or ways of life. These variations allowed the organisms to outcompete other organisms that belonged to the same species but lacked the favorable new variations. A bird with a slightly longer beak, for example, would be able to pluck insects from deeper cracks in logs

Darwin illustrated evolution with finches from the Galápagos Islands. These bird species all evolved from the same ancestor, but their beaks are adapted to different kinds of food, from hard seeds to tiny insects.

and tree trunks than the other birds could manage. This would give the longer-beaked bird an edge in survival.

Yet Darwin could not explain the mechanism of heredity—exactly how parents transmitted characteristics to their children, and how variations occurred in those characteristics. Not until the science of genetics developed in the twentieth century, bringing important discoveries about the roles of genes and eventually of DNA, did scientists grasp the mechanisms of genetic inheritance and genetic variation.

Work in Progress

Near the end of *On the Origin of Species*, Darwin wrote that when the world came to accept his findings there would be "a considerable revolution in natural history."[4] An understanding of evolution, he said, would not only enrich the sciences but would give people a whole new view of life—all forms of life. "Light," Darwin predicted, "will be thrown on the origin of man and his history."[5]

On the Origin of Species is not a short book (although it is a lot shorter than Darwin initially meant it to be). Yet that single sentence near the end of the book is Darwin's only mention of human origins. Darwin was well aware that many people would be disturbed by the idea that plant and animal species changed and evolved naturally, rather than receiving their complete and final forms through divine creation. But even some of those who could accept the evolution of plants and animals might reject the idea that human beings, too, were part of this natural process. Placing humans in the natural order would seem to go against religious traditions.

Although Darwin devoted just one sentence in *On the Origin of Species* to human origins, his readers had no trouble making the connection between evolution and humankind. Many of them, as he expected, were outraged. They were disgusted by the suggestion that humans had evolved from animals, and they found the possibility that human origins were natural rather than supernatural to be irreligious.

Despite initial ridicule and scorn, such as this nineteenth-century sketch of Darwin as an orang-utan, evolution won scientific acceptance and is now recognized as the foundation of biology.

Others, convinced by Darwin's mass of evidence, accepted the reality of evolution in the natural world. Many of these readers recognized that evolution applies to humans just as it applies to other forms of life, and they were able to reconcile the new concept with their religious beliefs.

In 1871 Darwin tackled the ticklish subject of people and evolution head-on in a book called *The Descent of Man*. It was one of the early steps in an investigation of human origins that is still going on today.

Although the fact of evolution is now established beyond reasonable scientific doubt, much remains to be learned about how it occurs. As part of the scientific process, experts constantly examine new evidence. This frequently leads them to revise or fine-tune their ideas about the mechanisms of evolution and also about the rate at which speciation, or the emergence of new species, takes place. Evolutionary scientists now know that natural selection is not the only factor that influences the development of new species. Climate change, movements of populations, inbreeding, and random chance also play a role in speciation. One lively area of modern evolutionary research, for example, is population genetics, which studies the different ways that genetic variations occur and spread in populations of different sizes, including human populations.

"The proper study of mankind is man," wrote the British poet Alexander Pope in the 1730s.[6] People of all times and cultures have speculated about the nature and origins of humankind. In the modern world, science has allowed us to probe deeply into our own nature, yet where we came from and how we came to be what we are today remains a complicated puzzle. More pieces of the puzzle are missing than have been found, but each new discovery adds to the picture, even if the experts are not yet certain where it fits. For this work in progress, scientists use what has been called "a toolbox for human origins."[7] The tools in the toolbox are an array of techniques and skills that fall into three broad categories. One category is genetics, the study of how DNA and genes work. Another is paleoanthropology, the study of ancient human life through physical traces such as fossils and stone tools. The third category is evolutionary science, which looks at the big picture of evolution, with topics such as population genetics and natural selection.

Modern people—*Homo sapiens*, to use the scientific name for our species—are the only members of the human family that exist today. Yet during the past century and a half scientists have learned that over the span of millions of years, evolution has produced many other species of humans or close human relatives, all of whom are now extinct. In the years since Darwin wrote *On the Origin of Species*, discoveries such as Raymond Dart's meticulously cleaned fossil of the Taung child have thrown light, just as Darwin predicted, on the early stages of human evolution.

In this first volume of our series *Humans: An Evolutionary History*, you will read about the search for the earliest human ancestors—from the study of ancient apes to the discovery of the australopiths, a branch of the human family tree that flourished in Africa several million years ago. The second volume introduces several other branches of the family tree, including the first true humans. In volume three we focus on the Neanderthals and other human species that lived in Eurasia during the Ice Age. Lastly, in volume four, we look at the origins of modern humans and how they spread throughout the world. Together the four books tell the story of human evolution as it is known today. Before scientists could start to understand that story, however, they had to dispose of mistaken ideas and false expectations about human origins. Correcting those mistakes was a major step forward in evolutionary science.

ONE

Myths and Misconceptions

In Darwin's time, human evolution was not just new and controversial—it was much misunderstood as well, even among scientists who accepted the basic idea that humankind had been shaped by natural forces. Some experts searched for a "missing link" between apes and humans, not realizing that the creature they sought had never existed. Others pictured human evolution as a triumphant story of progress from "primitive" cavemen to "advanced" modern people. Gradually a clearer view of the human past emerged as fossils of early ancestors began to reveal their secrets. First, though, evolution itself had to be defended.

Huxley v. Owen

One of the most vigorous champions of Darwin's ideas was Thomas Henry Huxley, a British anatomist and biologist. Huxley read *On the Origin of Species* in 1859, right after it was published. According to some accounts, when Huxley had finished the book he said, "How extremely stupid not to have thought of that myself." [8] Huxley's support of Darwin—particularly Darwin's views on human evolution—soon brought him into conflict with one of the leading scientists in Britain, Sir Richard Owen.

Owen was both an anatomist and a paleontologist. Huxley had clashed with him before on the subject of the formation of the human skull. Owen had claimed that a skull started out as a vertebra, or piece of the backbone, that grew larger and took on new features as a fetus developed in the womb. Huxley disagreed and was able to show that the structure of a human skull is different from that of a vertebra, and that a vertebra could not develop into a skull. Huxley was right, but he had made an enemy of Owen.

After *On the Origin of Species* appeared, Owen rejected the idea of the evolution of species and declared that Darwin's work "would be forgotten in ten years."[9] Huxley, meanwhile, had written a very favorable review of the book for the *London Times*. Before long Owen and Huxley again clashed in a scientific disagreement, and this time the question concerned humankind's place in the natural world. Once again, their conflict was about the human head, although the focus was now on the brain rather than the skull.

At a scientific meeting at the University of Cambridge, Owen read a paper in which he claimed that the human brain is structurally different from the brains of apes.

Thomas Henry Huxley

He argued that certain physical features of the human brain set it completely apart from ape and monkey brains. Huxley, who was in the audience, stood up and stated that he could prove that Owen was wrong. In the scientific world, this bold confrontation was not unlike challenging someone to an intellectual duel.

Owen *was* wrong, as Huxley demonstrated in two 1861 papers. He showed that although there are differences in size and shape between human brains and the brains of gorillas and chimpanzees, human brains and ape brains consist of the same basic structures. Huxley's papers grew into a book that he published two years

Sir Richard Owen

later under the title *Evidence as to Man's Place in Nature*. In this work Huxley explored the many anatomical similarities between the skeletons and organs of human beings and the skeletons and organs of the animals that he considered to be the closest relatives of humans: the gorilla and the chimpanzee.

As science began to recognize that humans were evolutionarily linked to apes and monkeys, the notion also filtered into the public realm. Some people reacted with revulsion, scorn, bewilderment, or even humor. A bishop's wife was reported to have said, upon hearing the news, "Descended from the apes! My dear, let us hope that it is not so; but if it is, that it does not become generally known."[10] Cartoons appeared that showed monkeys wearing Darwin's highly recognizable long white beard. And amid the unease created by the idea of human evolution, misunderstandings took root.

The "Missing Link"

"Descended from the apes!" Whether the wife of the Bishop of Worcester ever really made that remark or not, the story was repeated many times, not just because it was funny but because the remark struck at the heart of what unsettled people about humans and evolution. Unfortunately, it was based on a misunderstanding.

Many people, including some scientists, thought Darwin had said that humans are descended from the kinds of apes that appeared in nineteenth-century circuses and zoos—gorillas, chimpanzees, and orangutans. These are the same great apes that exist today (although they are now threatened with extinction). Some people in Darwin's time found it impossible, or at least unpleasant, to look at such creatures and picture them giving rise to humans, however slowly and gradually the change might have taken place. Yet Darwin had *not* claimed that humans are descended from any species of ape or monkey known in the modern world. Darwin claimed that apes are cousins of humans, not their ancestors. Both apes and humans are descended from some unknown, long-extinct ancestor—an ancestor, however, that would in some ways have resembled an ape.

Descended from apes, or descended from an apelike ancestor? The difference may seem small, perhaps nonexistent. Yet the idea that people came directly from the familiar gorillas or chimpanzees seized the popular imagination. It supported the notion of a "missing link"—a creature partly ape and partly human that once must have existed, bridging the gap between the two.

A link is a unit in a chain, and the image of the missing link came from a view of life that modern historians of science have called the Great Chain of Being. In this view, which dates back to the Middle Ages, all living things were arranged in a ladder or chain from lowest to highest. Worms were on the bottom rung, for example, but even among worms there were "higher," more advanced types, and "lower," more primitive ones. Humans stood on the very top rung of physical beings, above the animals but below the angels.

Closely related to the Great Chain of Being was the notion of progress, a concept that shaped early thinking about evolution in general and human origins in particular. Scientists now know that evolution is not progressive—that is, it does not move toward a goal, such as from lower to higher life forms. Evolution simply happens, as chance and changing circumstances give rise to new species. For a long time, however, people thought of evolution in progressive terms, with each form of life as a stepping-stone on the way to a "higher" one.

In the progressive view of evolution, humans started their journey as apelike creatures. As they mastered various challenges, such as learning to walk upright and to use tools and fire, they gradually moved from their lowly state into a much higher state as civilized beings. This view formed the basis for hundreds of textbook illustrations and museum exhibits that showed humans evolving "upward" in a single straight line, from four-legged apes to stooped, shambling cavepeople to modern humans who stride forth upright.

In a 1993 book titled *Narratives of Human Evolution*, an anthropologist named Misia Landau pointed out that the progressive vision of human evolution was appealing because it resembled a myth or story in which the hero overcomes obstacles and achieves his goal. The reality, scientists now know, was far more complex. Human evolution did not proceed in a straight, unbroken line from apes to us. It unfolded in a cluster of parallel or overlapping offshoots that resemble the branches of a bush. Nor did evolution proceed from lower to higher forms, or from primitive to advanced ones. Each stage, in its time, was as advanced as it needed to be. In the late nineteenth century and well into the twentieth century, however, the progressive view of human evolution held sway, along with the notion of the missing link.

Clues from the Distant Past

The so-called link between ape and human was "missing" because no fossils or other traces of it had ever been found. In the late nineteenth century, the missing link became the object of a scientific manhunt—or, technically, an ape-man hunt.

Fossils of ancient people had already turned up in a few places. Three years before Darwin published *On the Origin of Species*, workers at a limestone quarry in Germany's Neander Valley had found part of a skull and some bones. (A lot of fossils have turned up in quarries, mines, and other sites where people cut or blast stone. Raymond Dart, the South African discoverer of the Taung child, was well aware of this fact, which is why he hoped to get some fossils from the Taung limestone quarry.) Although the German fossils were very old, they were recognizably human. Those fossils and others like them, today known as Neanderthals, could not be relics of an ape-man such as the missing link was believed to be.

Ernst Haeckel, a German physician and scientist who became an enthusiastic evolutionist, was convinced that fossils of a creature midway between ape and human were waiting to be discovered. He urged his students to go out and find them. In 1891 one of those students, Eugene Dubois, was digging on the island of Java in Southeast Asia when he found

Becoming a Fossil

The fossil record of past life on Earth is full of holes. Given the great number of plants and animals that have lived and died on the planet, fossils are fairly rare. That's because only in certain circumstances can a dead plant or animal become a fossil. Many dead organisms fail to meet the necessary conditions for future fossilhood.

Being eaten is a major obstacle to becoming a fossil. Plants that are eaten disappear when they are digested, although their seeds may survive in the droppings of the birds or animals that ate them, and the droppings may turn into fossils (fossilized feces are called coprolites). Animals that are eaten may be swallowed whole, or torn apart and carried off in pieces, or crunched to bits, bones and all, by animals with powerful jaws. Sometimes nothing remains. Sometimes bones remain, although they are likely to be broken and dismembered from the skeleton. Finding a complete or nearly complete fossil animal is a rare and exciting event in a paleontologist's life. Most fossil finds are single bones. Many of them are teeth, which are among the hardest and most durable bones.

Above: *Our human ancestors were likely to fall victim to predatory birds, making it difficult for them to become fossils. Here, a stuffed predator looms over a replica of the skull of the Taung child.*

If predators and scavengers do not entirely destroy a carcass, other threats await. Soft tissue decomposes, leaving bare bones that can be trampled by herds of grazing animals, cracked open by heat, or eroded by rain and windblown sand.

But if a body or a bone is quickly covered by sand, ash, or some other sediment, fossilization may take place. As water trickles through the sediment and the bone, it carries minerals from the sediment into the bone. The minerals gradually replace the organic matter of the bone, petrifying it, or turning it to stone. Even petrification does not guarantee that a fossil will be preserved. Winds or floods may expose the underground layer containing the fossil. Once in the open air, the fossil can be weathered and eroded.

An organism's best chance of becoming a famous fossil is to leave a tidy, undisturbed corpse that is immediately covered by a good preserving substance, such as sea-bottom mud, river silt, or volcanic ash. The sediment should contain high concentrations of minerals, but it should be low in acid, which dissolves bone. With luck, after a long time, the movement of the earth or wind, or a mining operation, will expose the resulting fossil at just the right time to catch the eye of a passing paleontologist.

Little Foot, a 2- to 3-million-year-old fossil, came to light in a South African cave.

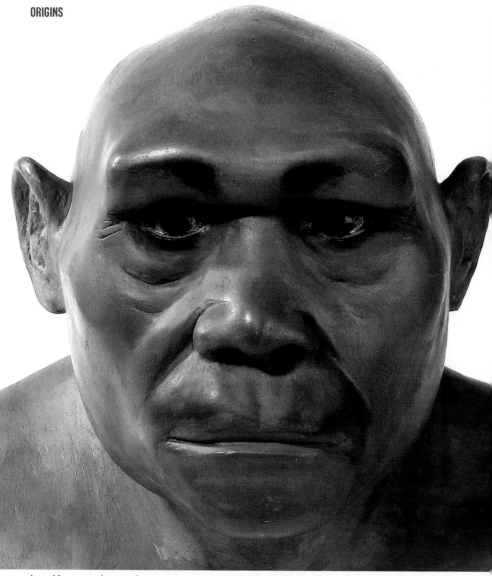

Java Man turned out to be an extinct human relative, not the "missing link" Dubois hoped to find.

the first of many fossils that, he claimed, came from "a great manlike ape."[11] For years Dubois insisted that his fossils were the missing link between apes and humans. The great majority of scientists disagreed. They concluded that Dubois's "Java Man" fossils were not as old as he claimed, and that they were human, not ape or ape-man. Even Haeckel, who had become embroiled in scientific controversies about fraud in his research, distanced himself from Dubois and Java Man. Dubois's finds, which are discussed in greater detail in the second volume of this series, are now known to come from a human species that lived much later than any possible missing link.

By 1920 scientists could examine dozens of European and Asian fossils of ancient ancestors. All of these fossils, however, were human. Clearly they had come from late stages in human evolution. And although Charles Darwin had predicted that people would be found to have evolved in Africa—the home of humankind's closest cousins, the gorillas and chimpanzees—no one had yet found human fossils on that continent.

In 1921 a window into the human past opened in Africa. Workers found an almost complete skull and some leg bones at the Broken Hill mine in what is now the nation of Zambia. The skull had thick, bony ridges above its eye sockets, yet its other features were much like those of modern human skulls. By measuring the cavity in the skull, experts determined that the brain had been as large as modern human brains. Like the earlier fossil finds from Europe and Asia, the Broken Hill remains appeared to come from a human who had not been dramatically different from *Homo sapiens*.

Three years later, when Raymond Dart found the Taung child in his box of rocks, he launched a new era in the study of human evolution. The Taung fossil clearly represented something much further back in evolutionary time than the Broken Hill fossil. Its brain was the size of an ape's brain, but its face and teeth were more humanlike than those of any known ape. Another significant feature of the Taung skull was the foramen magnum, the hole through which the spinal cord attaches to the brain. Apes walk on four legs with their spines behind their heads, sloping toward to the ground. The foramen magnum is at the back of their skulls. Humans, who walk upright with their spines below their heads, have the foramen magnum at the bottom of their skulls. When Dart saw that the Taung child's foramen magnum was at the bottom of its skull, he became convinced that he was looking at the remains of a creature that had been bipedal, or two-legged, and had walked upright.

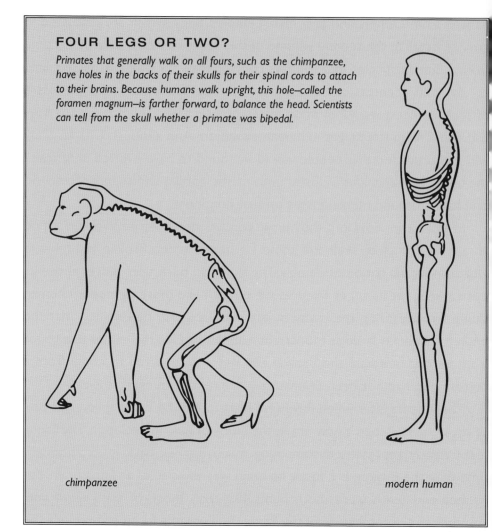

FOUR LEGS OR TWO?

Primates that generally walk on all fours, such as the chimpanzee, have holes in the backs of their skulls for their spinal cords to attach to their brains. Because humans walk upright, this hole—called the foramen magnum—is farther forward, to balance the head. Scientists can tell from the skull whether a primate was bipedal.

chimpanzee

modern human

Dart gave his find the scientific name *Australopithecus africanus*, which is Latin for "southern ape of Africa." The name may be poetic, but it did not reflect Dart's firm belief that the Taung child was neither ape nor human but an intermediate form between the two. Distinguished paleontologists, however, failed to share Dart's belief. Most of them dismissed the Taung child as the fossil of a strange or possibly deformed ape. It would take years, and many more fossil finds, for science to recognize the true significance of the Taung child. Dart's interpretation of the fossil would eventually be

AUSTRALOPITHECUS AFRICANUS

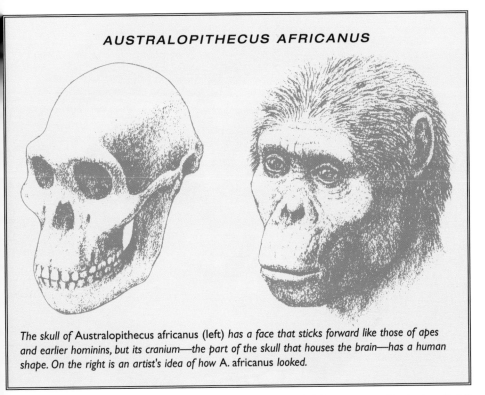

The skull of Australopithecus africanus (left) *has a face that sticks forward like those of apes and earlier hominins, but its cranium—the part of the skull that houses the brain—has a human shape. On the right is an artist's idea of how* A. africanus *looked.*

proved correct in many respects. Yet the Taung child was not a "missing link" in the sense that nineteenth-century scientists such as Haeckel and Dubois used the term—to refer to a bridge between the known species of apes and modern humans. The Taung child would turn out to be something very different: an early branch on the human family tree, but one that flourished long after the ancestors of apes and humans had separated.

This young chimpanzee is laughing—one of many forms of expression that we humans share with our closest living relatives.

TWO ⌒

Among the Primates

Science's first and most revolutionary insight into human evolution was the recognition that humans are part of the natural world. Humans are now known to be primates, members of a group of animals that also includes monkeys, apes, and a number of smaller creatures called prosimians, such as lemurs, tarsiers, and bush babies. The evolutionary story of humans begins with the origins of primates and their development over millions of years.

The Science of Names

Scientists use a system called taxonomy to classify and name living things. Traditionally, taxonomists sorted organisms into groups based on their differences and similarities. In these systems, humans occupied a family of their own within the primate order. Orangutans, gorillas, and chimps, together called the great apes, were grouped in a separate family. This reflected the long-standing belief that the great apes were more closely related to each other than any apes were related to humans.

Taxonomies are frequently revised, however. Today scientists who classify life forms are adopting an approach called phylogenetics, which sorts organisms into groups based on their evolutionary relatedness. Organisms are placed in the same taxon, or classification group, if they are descended from the same ancestor. As a result of this new approach, primate classification has changed in recent decades, reflecting new information about genetic closeness or distance among primates, including humans.

Recent genetic research has shown that humans and chimpanzees share the great majority of their genomes. In 2005 the U.S. Department of

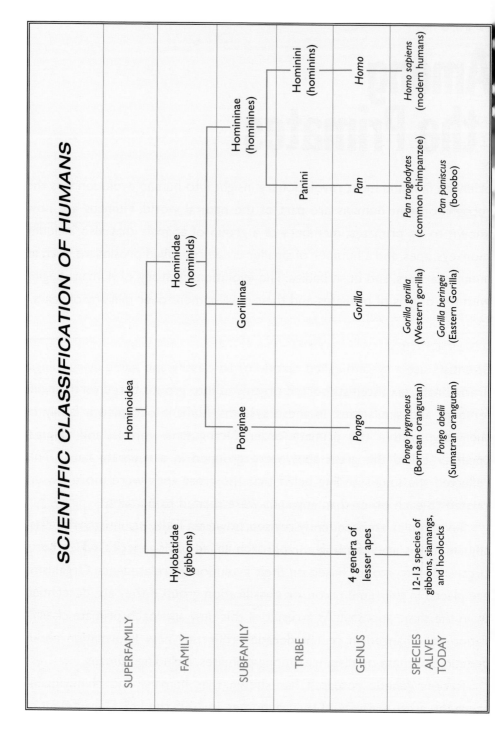

SCIENTIFIC CLASSIFICATION OF HUMANS

SUPERFAMILY	Hominoidea				
FAMILY	Hylobatidae (gibbons)	Hominidae (hominids)			
SUBFAMILY		Ponginae	Gorillinae	Homininae (hominines)	
TRIBE					Panini	Hominini (hominins)
GENUS	4 genera of lesser apes	Pongo	Gorilla	Pan	Homo
SPECIES ALIVE TODAY	12-13 species of gibbons, siamangs, and hoolocks	Pongo pygmaeus (Bornean orangutan) / Pongo abelii (Sumatran orangutan)	Gorilla gorilla (Western gorilla) / Gorilla beringei (Eastern Gorilla)	Pan troglodytes (common chimpanzee) / Pan paniscus (bonobo)	Homo sapiens (modern humans)

Health and Human Services National Institutes of Health (NIH) reported on the results of a study that had appeared in the scientific journal *Nature*. Chimpanzees, said the report, share 96 percent of the human gene sequence.[12] Although other researchers have come up with slightly lower or higher percentages of genetic overlap, scientists generally agree that chimpanzees and humans are more closely related to each other than either of them is related to gorillas or orangutans. The most current classification of apes and humans reflects this fact.

When talking about human evolution, scientists rely on key terms that come from taxonomy. When classifications change, the meanings of the terms can change, too. *Hominid* is a good example. In the 1960s, taxonomists recognized that humans and apes belonged to the same superfamily of primates, but they separated humans from apes by putting apes in the family Pongidae and humans in the family Hominidae. "Hominid" referred to humans and all of their fossil ancestors or possible fossil ancestors. The term became familiar, and many people, including some scientists, still use it that way today.

In the most current system of classification, however, *hominid* refers to living and extinct members of the family Hominidae, which includes humans *and* the great apes. Within the hominid family, humans and chimpanzees belong to the subfamily Homininae, or hominines. That subfamily is divided into two tribes, reflecting the split between chimps and humans.

One tribe, Panini, contains chimpanzees and their ancestors. Today this tribe is represented by two species in the genus *Pan*, the common chimp and the bonobo. The other tribe is Hominini, or the hominins. This tribe contains the species that evolved in the line of descent that separated from the apes. Humans and their ancestors are hominins, and so are the branches of this evolutionary line that died out, leaving no descendants in the modern world. The terminology may seem confusing, but paleoanthropologists do not talk very much about the hominines (with an e), the chimps-plus-humans subfamily. They are primarily interested in the hominins (without an e), the human tribe.

Only one species of hominin exists today: *Homo sapiens*, or modern humans. Other humanlike species existed in the past but are now extinct, and classifying some of these can be challenging. Modern humans, the only living hominins, belong to the genus *Homo*. As a result, any extinct species that scientists have placed in the genus *Homo* is unquestionably a hominin. Some of the biggest questions in paleoanthropology, however, concern humanlike species that belong to other genera. How do we classify them?

Everyone agrees that close human ancestors, such as the Neanderthals, belong to the tribe of Hominini. They are hominins. Paleoanthropologists have sometimes disagreed, though, on how to classify more distant ancestors, such as Raymond Dart's *Australopithecus africanus* and several much older fossils that combine apelike and humanlike features. These creatures were clearly hominids, members of the family that includes great apes and humans. But were they more closely related to humans or to apes? In considering that question, scientists draw on what they have learned about how apes and humans evolved as offshoots within the primate order.

Primate Roots

Paleontologists know less about the evolution of primates than about some other orders of mammals because primate fossils are comparatively scarce. One reason for the scarcity may be that the majority of primates have been arboreal, or tree-dwelling, and have lived in tropical or subtropical forests. In such environments, a carcass is seldom covered intact by mud, sand, or ash. Whatever is not consumed by predators and scavengers usually becomes buried in damp, acidic forest soil, which does not preserve bone well. Another reason for the scarcity of primate fossils may be that during certain periods of the distant past, primates themselves became scarce for a time. Despite gaps in the fossil record, however, paleontologists are piecing together a picture of primate origins and evolution.

The earliest forms of primates appeared around 60 or 65 million years ago, after the extinction of the dinosaurs opened up possibilities for mammals to fill newly vacant ecological roles. Primates probably developed from the small, arboreal, insect-eating early mammals that had existed alongside the dinosaurs.

During a period that geologists call the Eocene epoch, which lasted from about 55 to 34 million years ago, primates acquired the full set of features that set them apart from other mammals. Among these features are opposable big toes—which function like thumbs and allow primates to

Would it be useful to have four hands instead of two? Many primates have opposable toes that act like thumbs, letting these animals grasp things with their feet. Evolution, however, has removed that feature from humans.

grasp things—on all four feet; flat nails rather than claws on at least some of their digits; a brain that is large for their overall body size; and eyes that are large and set facing forward in the front of the face. The Eocene world was warmer than the modern world, with tropical temperatures and forests extending far north and south of the equator. The forest-dwelling primates spread throughout the world, with the likely exception of Australia and Antarctica, where no primate fossils have been found.

Scientists think that all of these early primates were arboreal. They moved around by jumping and by running along branches. Their main food was insects, although later some of them began eating plant foods. Most early primates were probably nocturnal, or active at night. Their eyes were bigger and their noses were smaller than those of the ancestral mammals, showing that the primates relied more on sight and less on scent.

About 40 million years ago temperatures on Earth began to cool. The lush forests disappeared from places like North America and Europe, and so did the primates. Only in Africa, which remained covered with thick trop-ical forests, did primates continue to flourish. New types of fruit-eating pri-mates evolved. Fossil deposits from Fayum, Egypt, show that North Africa had a large and diverse group of these species between 36 and 31 million years ago. Scientists think that the primates of this era were the ancestors of both monkeys and apes. By about 35 million years ago some primates—the ancestors of the New World monkeys—had reached the Americas. (The details of this migration are unknown, but primates could have been carried on floating logs or mats of vegetation across the Atlantic Ocean, which was narrower than it is now.) And by 20 million years ago a new kind of primate had evolved in Africa: the ape.

Ancient Apes

Several features set apes apart from other primates. Apes lack tails. Apes' elbow joints allow them to rotate their forearms far more than monkeys can (humans can do the same thing). Apes are generally larger than monkeys. Although they typically walk on four legs, as monkeys do, they can also walk upright on two legs, and they sometimes do this for short distances. These features did not appear all at once. Paleontologists trace their gradual appearance among various kinds of primates they call stem apes or apelike primates.

One of the oldest known candidates for apehood is *Proconsul.* Fossils of this primate, dating from around 20 million years ago, have been found in the East African nation of Kenya. *Proconsul* had both monkeylike and apelike features. Interestingly, the proportions of its hands—the length of the thumb relative to the fingers—were closer to those of humans than to apes. The scientific jury is still out on whether *Proconsul* was a true ape.

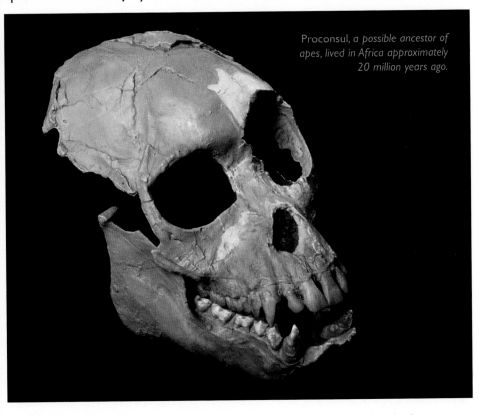

Proconsul, a possible ancestor of apes, lived in Africa approximately 20 million years ago.

By 17 to 15 million years ago, primates existed that paleontologists can definitely identify as apes. In fact, so many fossil apes are known from the

Does *Gigantopithecus* Live On?

The largest ape that ever lived once roamed the forests of ancient Asia. It came to light in 1935, when a German paleoanthropologist named Ralph von Koenigswald discovered a very large molar tooth from an unknown primate. At the time Koengiswald was browsing in a medicine shop in Hong Kong, knowing that fossils could often be found in such places, where they were ground up for use in traditional potions. Over the next several years Koenigswald found more huge primate teeth in Chinese pharmacies.

Koenigswald decided that his find must have been bigger than any known primate. He named it *Gigantopithecus*, or "giant ape." World War II broke out just then, and Koenigswald, who was working on the Southeast Asian island of Java, was captured by the Japanese. A friend hid the

Above: *Bill Munns, who has made primate models for both museums and movies, is dwarfed by his model* Gigantopithecus.

Gigantopithecus teeth, burying them in a milk jar in his backyard. After the war, Koenigswald retrieved the teeth, settled in New York City, and resumed his investigation of the giant fossil ape.

Since then scientists have found more *Gigantopithecus* fossils in China, India, and Vietnam. Most of the finds are teeth, but there are a few jaw-bones as well. Differences among them suggest that Asia may once have been home to several species of *Gigantopithecus*, probably related to *Siva-pithecus*. Estimates of the giant ape's size cover a broad range. Some experts think it may have been only a little larger than the largest pri-mates alive today, adult male silverback gorillas.[52] This would make Giganto about 6 feet tall (under 2 meters), with a weight of about 400 pounds (181.6 kilograms).[53] Others compare *Gigantopithecus* to a full-grown male polar bear: more than 10 feet (3 meters) tall and weighing 1,200 pounds (545 kilograms).[54] Either way, Giganto was a big ape.

Ever since the discovery of *Gigantopithecus*, people have speculated that small, isolated populations of this giant ape might still be alive. Could encounters with surviving Gigantos be the source of folklore about apemanlike creatures such as Yeti in the Himalayan region and Sasquatch or Bigfoot in North America? Not likely. For one thing, no proof exists that Yeti and Bigfoot are real. Wildlife experts say that it would have been extremely difficult for a population of such large mam-mals to escape scientific scrutiny into the twenty-first century.

The youngest Giganto fossils are hundreds of thousands of years old. But although *Gigantopithecus* is long extinct, the giant ape did coexist with early humans in Asia. At a site called Lang Trang in Vietnam, hominin and *Gigantopithecus* fossils occurred in the same layer of sediment, meaning that people and Giganto lived in the same place at around the same time. Did memories of ancient encounters get passed down through the ages to become folklore? Or, perhaps more likely, did people create the tales after stumbling upon scattered fossils of the extinct giant?

Miocene epoch, which began roughly 24 million years ago and lasted until almost 5 million years ago, that paleoanthropologist Roger Lewin has called the Miocene "the Age of the Ape."[13]

Many Miocene ape species have been found only in Africa, but apes migrated to other continents, where new species evolved. Fossil finds in China and Vietnam show that Sivapithecus, an ape that was probably the ancestor of orangutans, existed there by 17 million years ago. The earliest ape fossils from central and eastern Europe and Turkey date from about 14.5 million years ago. One of the most-studied European fossil apes is Dryopithecus, between 9 and 12 million years old. Some of its features resemble the very early Proconsul, some resemble Sivapithecus and the later orangutans, and some resemble the African apes. Ankarapithecus, known from two partial skulls discovered in Turkey in 1980 and 1996, also combines features of Sivapithecus and African apes, but its teeth are different from those of other fossil apes and humans. Like many creatures known from the fossil record, Ankarapithecus probably represents a branch of evolution that died out without leaving descendants in the modern world.

Over millions of years, some ape species became extinct and new ones appeared. Paleontologists do not have enough evidence to sort out the lines of descent that led from ancient apes to modern ones, much less to identify a particular fossil primate as the last common ancestor of apes and humans. They have, however, learned a great deal about the way apes lived in Africa during the late Miocene epoch, between about 5 and 10 million years ago.

By examining teeth (one of the commonest kinds of fossil), scientists can tell what type of diet an animal ate. Soft fruits, tough tubers, hard seeds and grains, and meat slashed or chewed from bone all leave characteristic marks on the surface enamel of the teeth. From other bones scientists can tell an animal's size, sex, and how it walked.

Fossil apes fall into two broad types. Some had smaller teeth with thinner enamel and shoulder joints that let them hang suspended from overhead branches. These suspensory apes, as scientists call them, probably moved about chiefly by swinging from branch to branch, as gibbons and some other primates do today. They ate fruits, lived in moist forests, and spent all or most of their time in trees. Fossils of species like this have been found in Africa, Europe, and Asia.

Quadrupedal apes, in contrast, are known only from Africa. These apes moved around mainly by walking on all fours, either along tree branches or on the ground. They had larger teeth with thicker enamel. They moved their jaws with powerful muscles that were attached to large jawbones, to protruding cheekbones, and even to bony ridges on their skulls. Their diet consisted of harder fruits and nuts, and possibly roots and bulbs. They lived in dry woodlands and spent some time foraging for food on the ground.

Around 7 million years ago, toward the end of the Miocene epoch, global temperatures began to cool again. Africa's tropical forests shrank somewhat. Open woodlands grew more extensive, and grasslands began to appear. In time these changes created the savanna landscape seen in parts of Africa today. New species of grass-eating animals evolved to graze on those grasslands.

The late Miocene epoch was also a significant time in human evolution. It was then that the line leading to chimpanzees and the line leading to humans separated, and the hominins were born.

11 July 2002

International weekly journal of scie

nature

www.nature.com/nat

The earliest known hominic

Sahelanthropus, *the oldest fossil yet found with humanlike features, was front-page news in the scientific world.*

THREE

The Great Divide

When Raymond Dart published his description of the Taung fossils, he estimated their age at 500,000 to 1 million years. In the 1920s, even half a million years seemed very far in the human past. Thanks to advances in geological and fossil dating, we now know that the Taung child lived between 2 and 3 million years ago. Fossils found recently in Africa are at least twice that old. As new discoveries are made, the moment when humanlike features first appear on the scene keeps getting pushed further back in time.

At some point in the past, the evolutionary line leading to humans separated from the line leading to chimpanzees. That point is the hominin horizon, the time when the tribes of Panini and Hominini diverged from the last ancestor they both shared, and hominins came into existence. When did it happen? Scientists have two ways to answer that question. One uses the fossil record. The other measures the differences between modern people and modern chimpanzees, looking for signs of the split between the two lineages.

The Fossil Record

Charles Darwin declared in the nineteenth century that the human race would be found to have evolved in Africa. Many scientists in the late nineteenth and early twentieth centuries disagreed, believing that the original home of humankind was Asia. Darwin was proved right, however, when Raymond Dart and others started finding very old humanlike fossils in Africa. Today paleoanthropologists who hope to uncover remains of the earliest human ancestors focus on Africa. Between 1974 and the early years of the twenty-first century, they have been rewarded with a string of discoveries, bringing to light the oldest fossils yet found of hominids, members of the family that produced great apes and humans. Of these hominids, some may be hominins—species that form part of the human lineage.

Sahelanthropus, "Human Fossil": The oldest known fossil with human-like features is also one of the most recent discoveries. It was found by Ahounta Djimdoumalbaye, a student at the University of N'Djamena in Chad, a country in north-central Africa. Djimdoumalbaye, a skilled fossil hunter, was part of a French-Chadian paleoanthropology team that had been excavating in Chad's Djurab Desert, part of a region of Africa known as the Sahel. The team had unearthed many animal fossils since 1994, but on July 19, 2001, Djimdoumalbaye found something that made news around the world.[14]

The new find was a nearly complete skull (minus the lower jaw) in which apelike and humanlike features were mingled. The short face, small teeth, and thick enamel of the teeth are humanlike, although these features also appear in *Oreopithecus,* an extinct primate that may be an early great ape. The brain was small (computer imaging later revealed the brain size to be between 360 and 370 cubic centimeters, which is less than average for the modern apes).[15] Yet the newly discovered skull had a prominent brow ridge or bulge of bone above the eyes, a feature seen in fossils that are known to be early humans. Its foramen magnum was at the bottom rather than the back of the skull—a likely sign of bipedalism, or upright walking.

The find received the scientific name *Sahelanthropus tchadensis,* meaning "human fossil from the Sahel in Chad." More familiarly, the skull came to be known as Toumaï, or "hope of life" in the Goran language of people who live in the Djurab Desert.

Sahelanthropus surprised the scientific world for two reasons. Only one other fossil of an early human ancestor had been found outside East or South Africa before this. *Sahelanthropus* was the second discovery of a possible human ancestor far from nearly all of the previous finds. It confirmed

An artist's vision of Toumaï at home in a fruitful landscape, now a North African desert

that the geographic distribution of humanlike forms had been broader than expected—and gave paleoanthropologists more places to search.

An even more surprising fact about *Sahelanthropus* was its age, which scientists have estimated on the basis of indirect evidence. The fossil was found at the same level as remains of animals such as early elephants, a large wild boar, and three-toed horses. Some of these remains resemble animal fossils from other sites in Africa. At those other sites, the animal fossils came from layers of volcanic rocks that can be dated to about 7 million years ago. If the similar animals at the *Sahelanthropus* site lived at the same time, then *Sahelanthropus* too would be 7 million years old. On the basis of this indirect evidence, the team that has studied *Sahelanthropus* estimates its age at between 6 and 7 million years, making it the oldest known fossil with humanlike features.

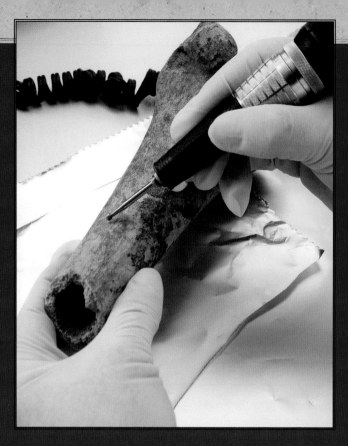

Dating Fossils

When someone finds a new fossil, one of the first questions asked is: how old is it? To form a picture of human evolution over time, paleoanthropologists must give dates to their fossil finds. How do they come up with the numbers?

There are two overall ways to date ancient fossils and other relics: absolute dating and relative dating. Absolute dating uses geological or chemical "clocks" to measure the time that has passed since a rock layer formed or since a plant or animal died. Relative dating compares layers of rock or sediment to determine whether one layer is older or younger than another. Absolute dating is like stating your age in years. Relative

Above: A scientist takes a sample from a human thighbone thought to date from the Middle Ages. Radiocarbon dating may reveal the bone's age.

{ 46 }

dating is like saying that you are older than your sister but younger than your brother.

Absolute dating depends on chronometric techniques, which measure physical changes that take place at known rates. The first technique to be developed was radiocarbon dating, or carbon-14 testing, but it is useful only on materials younger than about 40,000 years.[55] The best techniques for dating objects a million or more years old are potassium-argon dating, which measures the decay of potassium into argon in volcanic rocks, and a similar technique called argon-argon dating. If fossils are found with volcanic rocks, or just above or below them, dating the rocks can lead to a close estimate of the fossils' age.

Relative dating is based on the way layers of earth and rock are laid down. Younger layers are closer to the surface; older layers are deeper. The deeper a fossil is found, the older it is—unless, as is often the case, geological processes such as mountain building, earthquakes, and erosion have made the layers tilt, fold, wash away, or get mixed up in some other way.

The best kinds of relative dating go beyond depth measurements. They use markers, recognizable layers of sediment with known ages. One good source of markers is volcanic ash, which may travel on the wind across huge distances after large eruptions. A unique combination of chemicals gives the ash from each eruption a geochemical signature. If scientists find an ash layer at a new site and can tell from its signature that it came from the same eruption as a layer that has already been dated somewhere else, they can use the layer to date the new site. Another very useful kind of marker is the assemblage, the fossils of known plant and animal species found in the same deposit as a new fossil. If scientists already know the ages of any of those species, they can assume that the new fossil comes from about the same time. Standard practice for excavating a new fossil site is to determine the faunal age of each layer, which means identifying the fauna, or fossil animals, found there. This lets scientists compare the new site with sites of known age.

By the end of 2002 the team had discovered additional *Sahelanthropus* teeth and fragments of lower jaws. No body parts below the skull have been found. The search continues for additional fossils that may answer some of scientists' questions about *Sahelanthropus*. Was this animal truly bipedal? Was it related to other known species of early humanlike animals? Was it, perhaps, related to human ancestors?

Orrorin, "Original Man": Unlike the date for *Sahelanthropus*, the date for the second-oldest fossil with humanlike features is established by direct evidence. That fossil is *Orrorin tugensis*, found in the East African nation of Kenya.

In 1974, while excavating for fossils in an area called the Tugen Hills west of Lake Baringo in Kenya, a Kenyan-born paleontologist named Martin Pickford found a molar tooth from an unknown primate species. Pickford reported his find in the science journal *Nature* but did not have enough evidence to determine what it was.

Pickford was unable to resume work in the Tugen Hills until 2000, when he returned to the area as part of a French-Kenyan team. The team uncovered fossils that appeared to be related to the 1974 tooth: more loose teeth; two jaw fragments with teeth; part of an arm bone; and several finger bones. They also found two femurs, or thighbones. These are especially interesting because few post-cranial (below the head) fossils of hominids have been recovered. The scientists decided that their finds represented a new genus and species, which they named *Orrorin tugenensis* (*orrorin* means "original man" in the local language of the Tugen Hills).

Some of the *Orrorin* fossils were found between two layers of volcanic rock that could be dated. The layer below the fossils is about 6.2 million years old; the layer above them is 5.65 million years old. Researchers therefore estimate that *Orrorin* lived between 5.8 and 6 million years ago.[16]

Orrorin's teeth were more apelike than those of *Sahelanthropus*. The long, large canine teeth moved against other teeth called premolars in a way that sharpened the canines. This is an ape trait that appears to be missing from

Sahelanthropus. The most debated *Orrorin* fossils, however, are the femurs, which may show evidence of bipedalism.

Femurs connect at the upper end to the pelvis by means of the hip joint. The femur and pelvis, and the joint that connects them, are different in upright-walking humans than in apes. One difference is that ligaments that pass across the joint usually leave marks on human femurs but do not usually leave them on ape femurs. Researchers have found ligament marks on the *Orrorin* femurs—but that alone does not prove that *Orrorin* was bipedal, because such marks occur in some apes. Another difference is that the head of the femur, a ball-shaped knob that fits into a socket in the pelvis, bears more weight on its lower edge in humans—who carry all of their weight on two legs—than in animals that distribute their weight over four limbs. For

Orrorin's fossilized femur makes some experts think that this ancient primate walked upright on two legs.

this reason the bone is especially dense on the bottom part of the head of a human femur. The heads of the *Orrorin* femurs have high bone density on their bottom surfaces. Like the ligament marks, this bone density looks to some paleoanthropologists like evidence of upright walking. Unfortunately, baboons (which are monkeys) and some other primates that move around a lot on the ground have the same bone density pattern, so it is not absolute proof of bipedalism.[17]

Future fossil finds—perhaps feet and ankles—may help clear up the question of whether *Orrorin* moved on four legs or two. Perhaps, like chimpanzees today, it did both. Its habitat, judging by the remains of animals found with the *Orrorin* fossils, was a mix of forest, brushy woodland, and wet or swampy grassland such as a lake border.

Ardipithecus, **"Ground Ape":** The last of the very early humanlike fossils are two species of *Ardipithecus*, which lived in Ethiopia between 4.3 and 5.8 million years ago.[18] In 1992 paleontologist Gen Suwa was part of a twenty-person team looking for fossils in Aramis, a region of dry badlands in Ethiopia. Something on the ground caught Suwa's eye. "I knew immediately that it was a hominid," he later said. "And because we had found other ancient animals that morning, I knew it was one of the oldest hominids ever found."[19]

Suwa, paleontologist Tim White, and other experts on the team went on to find skull fragments, a jawbone and some teeth, and broken arm bones. Based on these fossils, they first identified their find as a new species of *Australopithecus*, the genus that includes the Taung child and other fossils. Later they decided that the Aramis fossils represent not just a new species but a new genus. They chose the genus name *Ardipithecus*, meaning "ground ape," and the species name *ramidus*, or "root" in the language of the region. A second species, called *Ardipithecus kadabba*, was later identified from other fossils, although some experts think that the differences between the two are not significant enough to make them separate species.

Like *Orrorin*, *Ardipithecus* seems to have inhabited an environment of brushy woodlands, wet grasslands, and swamps. It may have eaten mostly soft fruits, because it had thinner tooth enamel than *Orrorin*, and some features of its teeth match those of modern chimpanzees. What about bipedalism?

gorilla foot

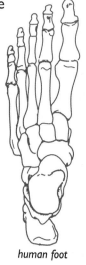

human foot

Apes have opposable big toes, like that on the gorilla foot. Human feet lack opposable toes, but they do a good job of supporting the weight of upright walkers.

The base of the *A. ramidus* skull fragment is too damaged to reveal whether the foramen magnum is in a humanlike or an apelike position. A single toe bone suggests that *Ardipithecus* could grasp things with its feet, as apes do, but might also have been able to flex its feet upward when walking, as humans do. In short, *Ardipithecus* is another mix of apelike and humanlike features. Its relationship to other hominids, and to human ancestors, is unknown.

Measuring the Chimp-Human Split

While paleoanthropologists comb dry riverbeds and sunbaked hillsides in search of clues to human origins, other scientists seek answers in a different kind of frontier: the molecular sciences laboratory. Instead of looking to fossils of long-dead hominids for answers, they have peered into the blood and DNA of living people and chimpanzees, with surprising results.

Immunological Responses: The first molecular studies on the divergence, or split, between humans and apes took place in the 1960s. These studies involved a process called the immunological response, which is a physical reaction that happens when an antigen from one organism is injected into another organism. An antigen is a protein. Bacteria, viruses, and pollen are common sources of antigens. In addition, the blood, saliva, and tissue of all species contain substances that act as antigens if injected into a different species. If a protein from species A is injected into species B, species B's immune system produces protective substances called antibodies to attack the antigens or defend against them. The formation of these antibodies is the immunological response. By measuring species B's immunological response to species A, scientists can determine the immunological distance between the two species—that is, how distantly or closely they are related.

In 1962 a Wayne State University researcher named Morris Goodman published the results of immunological tests he had performed on samples of the protein albumin from humans and the different kinds of apes. Goodman reported that the immunological distances were smaller among humans, chimpanzees, and gorillas than between any of those three and the Asian gibbons and orangutans. The study showed, in other words, that chimpanzees and gorillas were more closely related to humans than they were to orangutans and gibbons.

The results of Goodman's research were completely unexpected. For a long time, scientists had thought that the line of descent leading to humans had split away from the ape line before the apes diverged into African and Asian branches. In this view, humans had been separated from all apes for a long time. But Goodman's work indicated that humans and African apes had remained in the same line for some time after the Asian apes diverged onto their own line.

To determine when the human line had separated from the African apes, Vincent Sarich and Allan Wilson of the University of California at Berkeley again measured the immunological distances among humans, chimpanzees, and gorillas. They believed that immunological distance could serve as a kind of clock to measure how much time had passed since the species' ancestors diverged. To calibrate the clock, or set its measuring scale, they used the immunological distance between apes and monkeys. Based on the fossil record, scientists believed that the monkey-ape split took place 30 million years ago. This meant that the immunological distance between monkeys and apes was equal to 30 million years of separate evolution. Sarich and Wilson then compared the human-chimp-gorilla immunological distances to the monkey-ape distance. Their results, which they published in 1967, revealed that humans had split away from the African apes about 5 million years ago.[20]

Astonishment, not just surprise, greeted this announcement. Most experts had not dreamed that humans shared a common ancestor with apes as recently as 5 million years ago. The general view had been that humans split off from the ape line 15 to 20 million years ago. Many paleontologists thought that a fossil specimen called Ramapithecus, which had been found in Africa, Europe, and Asia, was an early human ancestor. *Ramapithecus*, however, was known to be about 14 million years old. If Sarich and Wilson were right, *Ramapithecus* had lived about 9 million years too early to be a human ancestor.

Dating with DNA: The rapid advance of genetic science in the 1980s and 1990s brought new molecular clocks that could measure the divergence time between species. With the ability to examine specific sequences, or strands, of DNA, researchers could count the differences between corresponding sections in the genomes of two species. Each difference represents a mutation, a variation in genetic structure that became a permanent part of the genome. A large number of differences between the two species' genomes meant that the species had been evolving on separate lines for a long time. A small number of differences meant that they had diverged more recently. As with the immunological clock, researchers calibrated the genetics clock by using divergences whose dates were known from the fossil record.

Several tests using genetic clocks have produced results fairly close to Sarich and Wilson's. A study that was

A December 2005 Science magazine cover illustrates key breakthroughs made in that year in genetic research. Several different species are represented on a model DNA molecule, including a stickleback fish, a chimpanzee, a fruit fly, and an influenza virus. Three members of Homo sapiens are represented, too, including Charles Darwin himself on the lower right.

reported in 2001, for example, found that gorillas split off from the chimp-human line about 7 million years ago, while chimps and humans diverged about 5 million years ago.[21] A study published in 2006 in the journal *Nature* produced similar results. Researchers compared the complete human and chimp genomes and cataloged the differences. Applying the molecular clock to their findings, they concluded that the human and chimpanzee lines separated between 6.3 and 5.4 million years ago.[22] (See book four of this series, *Modern Humans*, for a more detailed discussion of DNA and how researchers are using it to study the evolution of modern humans.)

Molecular clocks may not be entirely accurate. Scientists do not know for certain that mutation rates remain steady over time. Even if mutations do occur at a steady rate, factors such as population size or changes in breeding habits—a shift from short generations to longer ones, for exam-ple—can change the rate at which mutations spread through a species. Some paleoanthropologists, including Rob DeSalle and Ian Tattersall of the American Museum of Natural History, think that the human-chimp diver-gence probably took place closer to 7 million years ago. That date would include fossils older than 5 million years, such as *Sahelanthropus* and *Orrorin*, within the field of possible human ancestors.[23] But despite the need for caution, molecular clocks are a valuable tool for exploring human origins. They have told us that the human lineage is young, in evolutionary terms, and that our closest living relatives are the chimpanzees.

The researchers who published the 2006 *Nature* article may have dis-covered more evidence of the links between chimp and human ancestry. In their genomic study of the two species, they found signs that the female X chromosome in both humans and chimps is 1.2 million years younger than the other chromosomes. If they are right, humans and chimps inher-ited that chromosome from a common ancestor more than a million years after the first divergence between the human and chimp lines. In other words, the two lines interbred, producing hybrid offspring. Modern humans and chimps would have descended from the hybrid line. Geneticist James Mallet, who was not part of the research team, commented, "This [study] is contributing to the idea that species are kind of fuzzy. They become real over time, but it takes millions of years. We probably had a bit of a messy origin."[24]

Further research is needed to clarify and confirm the results of molecular-clock studies. Neither genomics researchers nor paleoanthropologists know the full significance of *Sahelanthropus* and the other very early fossils with humanlike features. They may be human ancestors. Or they may be apes that evolved bipedalism. Lines of hominid evolution could have branched off before, during, or after the human-chimp divergence and then died out, playing no part in the human story.

Long before Darwin and the advent of our modern research techniques, scientists were fascinated by the similarities between humans and chimps. Physicians who dissected the chimps found their internal structure almost identical to that of humans. The artist who made this engraving in 1748 clearly recognized the chimpanzee's humanlike qualities.

We now know that the lines of evolution leading to modern chimpanzees and modern humans split apart some 5 to 7 million years ago, but we do not yet know exactly what happened along each of those lines on the way to the present, or whether there were other lines that have since disappeared. Molecular studies can tell us only that the chimp-human split happened. Such studies cannot tell us where a particular fossil or group of fossils belongs on the human or ape

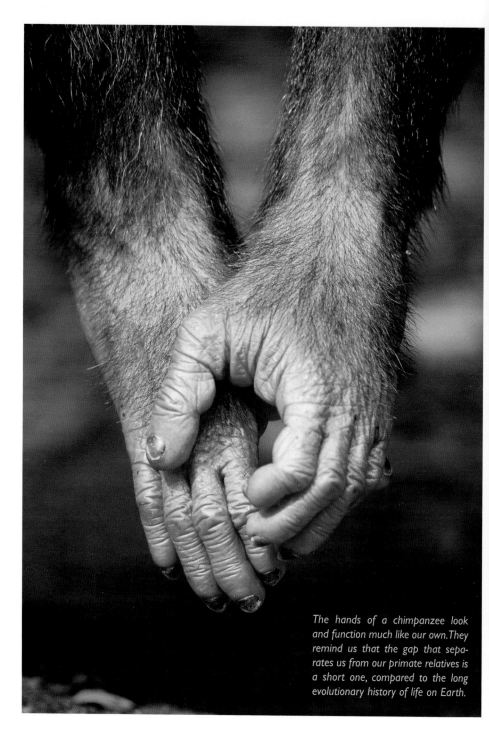

The hands of a chimpanzee look and function much like our own. They remind us that the gap that separates us from our primate relatives is a short one, compared to the long evolutionary history of life on Earth.

family tree. And even though the ancestors of humans and chimpanzees diverged a long time ago, the split did not mean that descendants in each line immediately took on clear-cut ape or human features. Apelike and humanlike features remained intermingled for millions of years as the two lines evolved slowly toward their present forms. That is why paleoanthropologists cannot always place their fossil finds clearly on either the ape or the human line.

Take the australopiths, for example. Although these hominids lived several million years after the chimp-human divergence, their fossils show a mix of ape and human features. Yet in spite of australopiths' many apelike features, most experts now consider them to be not just hominids but also hominins, members of the human evolutionary line. Raymond Dart's Taung child was the first australopith to be discovered, but the best-known australopith is a hominin superstar, the world's most famous 3.2-million-year-old woman.

Lucy, who lived in Africa more than 3 million years ago, seems to gaze questioningly upon the modern world in this life-sized model.

FOUR
Lucy and Her Kin

"It's no good being in front if you're going to be lonely," Raymond Dart once said.[25] Dart had learned the hard way that in science as in many other pursuits, the explorers and pioneers who lead the way can sometimes find themselves alone, waiting for the rest of the world to catch up with them.

When Dart claimed in the mid-1920s that the Taung fossil skull and brain represented an early human ancestor from southern Africa, he received little support from most of the scientific community. Many experts thought that *Australopithecus africanus*, as Dart named his find, was too old and too apelike to be connected with humankind. The paleontological mainstream was convinced at the time that human origins were to be sought in Asia. Dart's fossil was merely a curiosity.

Fortunately, Raymond Dart lived to the ripe old age of ninety-five. By the time he died in 1988 he had witnessed a series of spectacular discoveries that proved that he (and Darwin) had been right all along: Africa was indeed the human birthplace.

Mrs. Ples and *Paranthropus*

Dart's only strong supporter in the early years was Robert Broom, a Scottish-born surgeon who had taken up paleontology after moving to South Africa. One of Broom's most significant achievements was finding fossils in the Karoo region of South Africa. By identifying these fossils as mammal-like reptiles, Broom provided a crucial chapter in the growing body of knowledge about how mammals evolved from reptiles.

Broom was so excited by news of Dart's discovery that he rushed off to view the Taung child. Dart later recalled that Broom "burst into my

Robert Broom

laboratory unannounced. Ignoring me and my staff, he strode over to the bench where the skull reposed and dropped to his knees 'in adoration of our ancestor.'"[26] Broom did more than admire Dart's find. He wanted to discover australopiths, or fossils like Dart's—and he did so, in a way that was similar to Dart's experience.

In 1936 Broom heard that fossils were turning up at a limestone quarry at a place called Sterkfontein, near Broom's home in South Africa's Transvaal Province. Broom asked the foreman of the lime works to save fossils for him, and a few days later the foreman handed over a lump of rock that Broom recognized as an endocranial cast. It was a fossilized model of a brain very much like the one Dart had received from the Taung lime works. Broom hurried to the quarry, dug through the pile of blasted rock, and found pieces of a skull. He was certain that he had found the remains of an individual related to Dart's *Australopithecus*. Two years later, however, he decided that the Sterkfontein individual was different enough from the Taung specimen to deserve its own genus and species. He called it *Plesianthropus transvaalensis*, "near-man from the Transvaal."

Broom excavated other *Plesianthropus* fossils from Sterkfontein. There, in 1947, he and fellow paleontologist John Robinson made an especially exciting find: a nearly complete skull. It was smaller than the 1936 *Plesianthropus* skull. In many ape species, males are significantly larger than females, and Broom thought that the same might be true of *Plesianthropus*. He suggested that the new skull could have come from a female. The fossil soon gained the nickname Mrs. Ples, and although there is no proof that the skull is female, the name is still alive. (In 2004, viewers voted Mrs. Ples into ninety-fifth place on a "100 Greatest South Africans" list created by a South African television station.[27])

A handful of pocket change and some candy had already helped Broom discover a strikingly different kind of ancient hominid. In 1938 Broom had gotten word that a schoolboy named Gert Terblanche had found fossil teeth at Kromdraai, not far from Sterkfontein. Broom went to Gert's school and had the principal bring Gert to him. It so happened that Gert had carried four fossil teeth to school in his pockets that day, and the paleontologist managed to buy all four of them from the boy. Broom then asked Gert to show him where he had found the teeth, but before he could take the boy out of school Broom had to treat the students to a talk about finding fossils. Finally Gert led Broom to the hillside where he had found the teeth. The boy later traded his last fossil tooth to Broom for five chocolate bars.

Broom recovered skull fragments from the hillside, along with parts of a jawbone, an ankle bone, and an elbow bone. As he pieced together a partial skull from his fragments and Gert's teeth, he saw with surprise that it differed noticeably from both *Australopithecus* and *Plesianthropus*. The bone of the new skull was thicker, the teeth were larger, and the jaw was heavier. The cheekbones projected very far forward. The skull also had a sagittal crest, a ridge of bone running from front to back across the top of the skull. Marks on the cheekbones and the sagittal crest showed that powerful jaw muscles had been attached to them. Broom gave this discovery the scientific name *Paranthropus* ("like man") *robustus* ("strong" or "sturdy").

Teeth of Paranthropus, *a species that discoverer Broom regarded as "like man".*

Dart's Triumph

While Robert Broom hunted for fossils in and around Sterkfontein, Raymond Dart began a series of excavations at a place called Makapansgat, north of Johannesburg. Fossils of baboons and other animals had turned up in limestone caves there, and Dart thought that the caves might hold australopith remains. In the late 1940s he and his team found fossils at Makapansgat that Dart believed came from a new species of *Australopithecus*. Today, however, experts consider them to be *Australopithecus africanus*, the same species as the Taung child.

When Dart had introduced the Taung child to the world in the 1920s, the famous British anatomist Sir Arthur Keith had refused to consider the fossil even partly human. By 1947, though, Keith could no longer ignore the growing pile of evidence. The fossils that Dart, Broom, and others had found in South Africa clearly represented something more than apes. Keith declared:

When Professor Dart . . . claimed a human kinship for the juvenile australopithecine, I was one who took the view that when the adult form was discovered it would prove to be nearer akin to the living African anthropoids, the gorilla and chimpanzee. . . . I am now convinced that Professor Dart was right and I was wrong.[28]

Sir Arthur even went so far as to suggest a new name for the South African fossils. He thought they should be called Dartians, to rhyme with "Martians." The name did not catch on.

For *Australopithecus*, South Africa had been only the beginning. A few decades after Keith acknowledged the "human kinship" of the australopiths, discoveries in East Africa captured attention around the world.

Into Ethiopia

East Africa started making paleoanthropological news in the mid-twentieth century. In 1931 a Kenyan paleoanthropologist named Louis Leakey began excavating for traces of ancient humans at a place called Olduvai Gorge in northern Tanzania. Leakey was later joined by his wife, Mary, a skilled fossil finder who made many major discoveries, including the first fossil ever found of *Proconsul*, the earliest known primate that may be identified as an ape. In time the Leakeys' son Richard became a paleoanthropologist and museum administrator and also took a key part in East African hominin studies.

In the 1950s the Leakeys made several major finds at Olduvai: fossil teeth and a skull that they believed came from a previously unknown human ancestor. They dubbed this find *Zinjanthropus boisei*, or Zinj. The announcement of these discoveries swung the attention of the paleoanthropological world toward East Africa, and researchers from many countries started planning expeditions to dig there. The Leakeys, meanwhile, continued to work at Olduvai and a nearby site called Laetoli. They discovered fossils from human ancestors in the genus *Homo*, hominins that had lived closer to

Louis and Mary Leakey, shown here at work in 1961, spent years sifting the sands of East Africa in search of fossils.

the present than the South African australopiths. The full importance of these *Homo* fossils, which were the Leakeys' major contribution to paleoanthropology, belongs to the second volume in this history of human evolution. The interest that the Leakeys awakened in East Africa, however, led to a breakthrough in our knowledge of the australopiths.

In 1967 a joint Kenyan-American-French expedition began excavating in southwestern Ethiopia along the Omo River, which flows into Kenya's Lake Turkana. The scientists went to Omo every year to do field work—digging for more fossils. After a few years a new member joined the American team. He was Donald Johanson, an American graduate student who was working on his PhD degree.

Johanson was writing his doctoral dissertation on the subject of chimpanzee teeth, but he was deeply interested in hominid and hominin fossils. The Leakeys' discoveries in Tanzania had enthralled him. "I was still in high school when I read about Zinj in the *National Geographic*," Johanson later wrote. "The name Olduvai, with its hollow sound, rang in my head like a struck gong. . . . I began thinking more and more about anthropology. Leakey's experience was proof that a man could make a career out of digging up fossils."[29]

After several years of field work at Omo, Johanson helped organize a French-American team to work in northern Ethiopia in a region called the Afar triangle, a place where continental plates grind against each other. Over the ages, this geological activity has caused the earth to rise and fall and crack open, exposing layers of ancient rock. The expedition site was a place called Hadar, a hot, dry region of bluffs, gulches, and badlands, "all of them seeming to ooze fossils," Johanson wrote, adding, "It was a place paleontologists see only in their dreams."[30]

During the first field season at Hadar, in 1973, the team collected numerous fossils such as teeth from ancient pigs. Johanson was disappointed by the absence of hominid remains. Then, near the end of a day of surveying, he found three pieces of bone lying close together on the ground. They joined together perfectly and proved to be a knee joint with portions of the thighbone and shinbone. At first Johanson thought he was holding the knee of an ancient monkey. Then he saw that the way the joint fit together required the thighbone to angle slightly outward from the knee toward the hip. He knew at once what that meant.

Monkeys' and apes' thighbones point straight down. The legs of these primates never come directly under the animals' centers of gravity, which is why chimpanzees have a waddling gait when they occasionally walk on their hind legs. But in a human leg, the thighbone slants inward slightly from the hip to the knee, bringing the legs under the body's center of gravity during a stride.

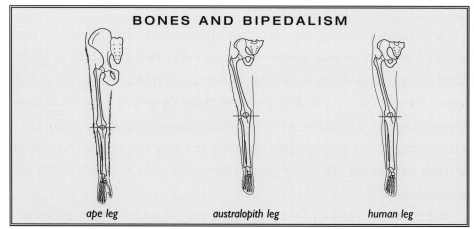

BONES AND BIPEDALISM

ape leg   australopith leg   human leg

Donald Johanson's exciting discovery of a knee joint suggested that australopiths walked upright. The angle of the thighbone between hip and knee in an australopith (center) is closer to that of a bipedal human (right) than to that of a quadrupedal ape (left).

The knee joint in Johanson's hand would not fit together with the thighbone straight, so there was only one possible conclusion. He had found the knee joint of something that walked upright like a human. Based on this sign of bipedalism, Johanson felt certain he was holding a hominin fossil.

Johanson's discovery was the first hominin knee joint ever found. The most remarkable thing about it was its age. Johanson and Maurice Taieb, the expedition's French geologist, estimated the age of the knee based on the geological interpretation of the strata, or layers of rock and sediment, around it. The joint was evidence that hominins had walked erect about 3 million years ago.

"Something Terrific"

The hominin knee joint was the most spectacular find of the first season at Hadar. Johanson and the others returned to the site in 1974. Alemahayu Asfaw, an Ethiopian member of the expedition, created considerable excitement when he found some hominin jaws. A few days later, Johanson planned to spend the afternoon doing paperwork in his tent, but Tom Gray, another member of the expedition, needed help pinpointing a location he was supposed to map. Johanson decided to let the paperwork wait and go with Gray to that part of the site. "When I got up that morning," he explained later, "I felt it was one of those days when you should press your luck. One of those days when something terrific might happen."[31]

Something did. Gray and Johanson spent several hours walking slowly across the uneven area of sand and gravel, searching the ground for fossils. The temperature was close to 110 degrees Fahrenheit, and the two men were ready to quit and head back to camp four miles away, when Johanson led the way into a small gully. He spotted an arm bone lying on the slope. Gray thought it was a monkey's arm. Johanson was sure it was hominin. Then he spotted part of a skull and, a few feet away, a thighbone. Gray spotted some ribs.

The two men looked around them in awe. The ground was littered with small brown hominin bones. There were vertebrae and a pelvis; the large

{ 67 }

pelvic opening for the birth canal showed that this bone had come from a female. Johanson and Gray realized that they could be looking at something extremely rare in paleoanthropology: a fairly complete set of fossilized remains from a single individual.

They marked the location of the find on their map and drove back to camp, spreading the news to other expedition members as they went. That afternoon everyone in camp went to the gully. Painstakingly they divided the site into sections, getting ready for a large-scale collecting task. That night the camp was, as Johanson puts it, "rocking with excitement."[32] No one went to bed. People sat under the stars and talked for hours. Full of high spirits, they played the Beatles song "Lucy in the Sky with Diamonds" again and again at full volume. By the end of the night the fossil hominin had become Lucy, and that has been her name ever since, although her official label in the collection of Hadar fossils is AL 288-1. (Lucy's discoverers and other scientists eventually decided that she belonged to the genus *Australopithecus* but was a separate species from the South African *A. africanus* fossils. They chose the species name *afarensis* for Lucy and the hominins like her whose remains have been collected at Hadar and other sites in the years since 1974.)

It took Johanson and the other expedition members three weeks to collect all the fossils from the Lucy site, combing through every bit of gravel to make sure they missed nothing. In the end they had recovered enough bones—and, in many cases, small fragments of bone—to add up to about 40 percent of a skeleton. Anatomists examined the remains and estimated that when Lucy was alive she had stood 3.5 feet (a little more than a meter) tall and weighed approximately 70 pounds (32 kilograms). Her brain was about the size of a chimpanzee's brain. She had long arms, with long fingers that were hooked like those of apes. Her pelvic bone, however, was shorter and broader than a chimpanzee pelvis—it was shaped more like a human pelvis.

Like other australopiths, Lucy is a mix of apelike and humanlike features. In life she would have looked—and almost certainly acted—much more like an ape than like a human. Her most humanlike feature, and the reason that many experts consider her to be a hominin as well as a hominid, is the strong suggestion from her pelvis and leg bones that she could walk erect on two legs. Further indications that australopiths were bipedal soon came from Laetoli in Tanzania.

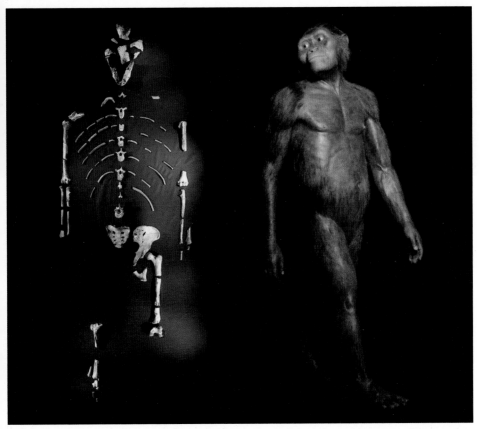

Lucy's discoverers found 40 percent of her skeleton (left), enough to serve as the basis for a full-scale reconstruction of this East African australopith.

Tracks Across Time

The Afar region, where Lucy was found, lies along Africa's Great Rift, which is part of a network of faults and fissures between Earth's continental plates. The rift system stretches southward from the Middle East along the eastern side of Africa to the coastal country of Mozambique. In East Africa, some sections of the rift zone contain lakes, swamps, and volcanoes or extinct

The Great Rift Valley is dotted with volcanoes like this one located in the East African nation of Djibouti. Ash belched forth from these volcanoes helped preserve some of the most important fossils in the human family tree.

volcanoes, good sources of sediment and ash for making fossils. Geologists know that in the distant past such conditions were common over much of the Great Rift.

Afar is not the only place along the rift zone where earth movements have brought ancient layers of sediment to the surface. As wind and water flow across these sediments, new fossils are continually revealed. Many important fossil finds besides Lucy, including *Ardipithecus*, have come from sites strung along the rift zone. Among those sites are Olduvai and Laetoli in northern Tanzania, where the Leakey family worked for many years.

In 1976 Mary Leakey led a team of scientists and excavators to Laetoli for field work. One afternoon, during a break, a couple of team members started horsing around, throwing chunks of dried elephant dung at each other. Paleoanthropologist Andrew Hill was searching for a piece of dung to use as ammunition when he noticed an exposed layer of old ash in a dry streambed. Dents in the ash looked like footprints. Excavation of the ash layer got under way the following year. The team found a number of bird and animal tracks and some that looked like the prints of upright-walking hominins. A major excavation effort in 1978 uncovered unmistakable hominin prints that had been preserved by a combination of perfect circumstances.

Near Laetoli is a volcano called Sadiman. Today, its fires quenched, it is extinct. Around 3.6 million years ago, though, Sadiman was active. It belonged to an unusual class of volcanoes called carbonitite volcanoes, which produce magma and ash with high amounts of calcium and magnesium carbonate. One day Sadiman shot out a burst of carbonitite ash, which has a texture like fine sand. A layer of ash blanketed the area. Rain fell afterward, just enough to dampen the ash and turn it into something that for a few days resembled wet cement. As creatures crawled, hopped, or walked across this surface, they left tracks behind. Those tracks dried in the sun and hardened. Then Sadiman belched forth more ash, sealing the tracks in a layer of soft rock that geologists call volcanic tuff. Eventually deposits of ash, sediment, and windblown soil covered the area. Hills and streams formed. Later still the surface eroded, exposing layers of tuff, one of which contained the tracks.

When the excavators on Mary Leakey's team scraped away grass and earth to uncover more of the tuff, they found a snapshot of activity that took place more than 3.5 million years ago. The tiny tracks of millipedes crisscrossed the unmistakable trails of birds, including large ostriches. Marks left by the feet of pigs, elephants, rhinos, giraffes, hares, and antelopes were easy to identify. And there, amid the confusion of animal tracks, were footprints that looked strangely familiar—not too different from our own. They were the tracks of two hominins, side by side, in a straight line. The workers followed the trackway until that layer of tuff vanished where it had eroded away. In all, the trail extended 77 feet (23.3 meters).

In the years since the Laetoli trackway was excavated, researchers have put forward many theories about what it represents. At first, Mary Leakey speculated that the tracks were made by hominins fleeing the volcanic eruptions. This, however, cannot be proved. No signs of running or panic are visible in any of the tracks, hominin or animal. In addition, birds that could have

Few relics of the past have sparked more speculation than this trail of footprints at Laetoli. Were they made by an australopith family? We will never know. The tracks on the right are from an extinct three-toed horse.

flown away continued to walk about on the ground. Others have suggested that the tracks were made by a male-female pair, or that one of them may have been carrying an infant (because some of the tracks appear slightly deeper than others), or that a third individual followed the first two, stepping in the tracks left by one of them (because some of the tracks appear to have partial double outlines).

These ideas appeal to our hunger for insight into our ancestors' lives, but there is not enough evidence to support them. All we know for certain from the tracks is that two individuals, one larger than the other, walked across the wet ash. Each walked upright on two feet. We do not know whether they were male or female, or even whether they walked together.

Most paleoanthropologists agree that the Laetoli tracks were made by hominins. The most likely candidate is Lucy's species, *Australopithecus afarensis*. Not only did *A. afarensis* live at the right time to make the tracks, but teeth and jaws from the species have been found at Laetoli.

Owen Lovejoy, a paleoanthropologist and anatomist who serves as a forensic science consultant and has done research on *A. afarensis*, has compared the Laetoli tracks to both chimpanzee and human footprints. A chimp's print clearly shows the big toe pointing outward at an angle from the foot. In a human print, the big toe is lined up with the other toes. Human feet also have prominent heel bones to help support the body, as well as arches on the bottom of the feet to absorb energy when the foot hits the ground. In Lovejoy's view, the Laetoli tracks show these features. "That's the kind of fine-tuning that you'd expect in a biped that had been that way for a very long period of time," he says.[33] He thinks that the australopiths that made the Laetoli tracks were full-time upright walkers, which would mean that bipedalism was already well developed by 3.6 million years ago.

Paleoanthropologist Tim White, who helped excavate the trackway in 1978, agrees that the tracks show clear humanlike features. "Make no mistake about it," he has said. "They are like modern human footprints."[34] More recently, however, a few experts have argued that the details preserved in the

Footprints for the Future?

When Mary Leakey finished excavating the Laetoli trackway in 1979, she and her team reburied the trackway, covering it with layers of plastic film, sand, and boulders to protect the fragile volcanic tuff. Their goal was to prevent the Laetoli tracks, the oldest known footprints of bipeds who may be human ancestors, from being destroyed by rain, wind, or the hoofs of grazing animals. Scientists who wanted to study the tracks would have to rely on photographs and molds such as plaster casts, made before the reburial.

Above: A conservation expert studies the Laetoli trackway in 1995, during a preservation project.

By the early 1990s, rain was eroding the sand, termites had eaten much of the plastic, and plant roots were threatening to penetrate the tuff and destroy the trackway. The Tanzanian Department of Antiquities and the Getty Conservation Institute (GCI), an American museum organization, created a plan to rebury the tracks under insect-resistant synthetic material, with capsules of time-release herbicides to kill intruding plants. Mary Leakey, eighty-three years old and living in Kenya, went to Laetoli in 1996 for a last look at the tracks before what was expected to be a permanent burial. "You've got to bury it," she said, "if you want to conserve it."[56]

In early 2008, however, the international scientific community heard alarming news about the Laetoli site. Charles Musiba of the University of Colorado at Denver reported, "The protective blanket over the prints is already breaking up. Unless something is done within the next five years, the site is going to suffer serious irreparable damage."[57]

One proposal is to construct a protective building, possibly a museum, over the trackway. Laetoli lies in a remote and rugged part of Tanzania, however, and building and guarding a structure there would be costly. Few people would be able to visit it. Several paleoanthropologists have proposed cutting the entire trackway out of the hillside and moving it to a museum in Dar es Salaam, the country's capital. A stroke  of enormous good luck preserved the footprints in the ash from Sadiman volcano. Perhaps the footprints will be lucky enough to be preserved again.

Above: *Mary Leakey, shown working at Laetoli in 1978, witnessed both the excavation of the site and its sealing in 1996.*

tracks are not fine enough to demonstrate a fully human footprint or stride. Their position is that we cannot be absolutely certain that A. *afarensis* made the tracks or even that the makers of the tracks were full-time bipeds, although the evidence leans that way.[35]

A Discovery at Dikika

Lucy is no longer the only *Australopithecus afarensis* superstar. She now shares the limelight with a remarkable find from Dikika, an Ethiopian site in the Afar triangle, across the river from Hadar where Lucy came to the surface.

Paleoanthropologist Zeresenay Alemseged led a team of his fellow Ethiopian scientists into the region in 1999. The following year an expedition member named Tilahun Gebreselassie spotted a fossil face looking out at him from the side of a hill. It was no bigger than a monkey's face, but it had small teeth and a smooth, unridged brow. It proved to be a young female

Ethiopian paleoanthropologist Zeresenay Alemseged spent five years uncovering the remains of this three-year-old female australopith, known as Selam.

A. *afarensis*, estimated to have died at the age of three about 3.3 million years ago.

Unlike Lucy, the Dikika child was not spread around in fragments that had to be assembled. Instead, the bones were encased in breccia, the same cementlike sandstone that Raymond Dart had picked out of the Taung child's skull with a knitting needle. The Dikika child may have died in or near the river and been buried by sand and pebbles before the corpse could be scavenged or degraded.

It took Zeresenay five years, working with precision tools such as dental drills, to remove the breccia from the skeleton "grain by grain," as he puts it.[36] When he was finished, the Dikika find—known in Ethiopia as Selam— was a partial skeleton that is about as complete as Lucy. She has most of her skull, including all of her milk teeth, with her permanent teeth embedded below them in her lower jaw. She also has both shoulders, part of her spine, several ribs, part of her right arm, and parts of both legs. Some fingers and a foot are also preserved. So is the hyoid bone, a fragile structure in the neck that is missing from most fossils. The hyoid bone was a necessary evolutionary development far back on the road to human speech, but its presence does not mean that A. *afarensis* had language—chimpanzees have hyoid bones, too, and Selam's is not much different from a chimp's. Overall, Selam gives scientists some skeletal parts that Lucy lacks. "But the most impressive difference between them," Zeresenay says, "is that this baby has a face."[37]

Selam's face was flat and projected outward from the skull, as a chimpanzee's does. Her brain had a volume of 330 cubic centimeters, making it about the same size as a three-year-old chimpanzee's brain. Her finger bones were longer than a human child's and curved like a chimpanzee's, and her shoulder blades resembled those of a young gorilla. Like other australopiths, though, Selam had a humanlike lower body. Her leg bones, including a tiny kneecap, are more evidence that australopiths walked upright. The Dikika child, like the Taung child decades earlier, has given us a wealth of information about the australopiths.

FIVE ⌒

An Abundance of Australopiths

Since Raymond Dart's discovery of the Taung child fossils in 1924, *Australopithecus* fossils have come to light in various places in both South Africa and East Africa. Scientists now believe that the genus *Australopithecus* evolved in Africa around 4.5 million years ago. It may have evolved from the earlier "ground ape" *Ardipithecus*, or it may have descended from some yet unknown ancestor.

Australopiths existed for more than 2 million years before disappearing from the fossil record. At times during their span of history, more than one australopith species existed in Africa, just as more than one species of chimpanzee exists today. Many scientists think that humans evolved from one of these australopith species, although this is not known for certain.

The Challenge of Classifying Ancient Hominins

The taxonomy or scientific classification of australopiths has changed many times over the years, and it will surely do so again. There is no universal agreement among paleoanthropologists about how these fossils should be classified. The difficulty lies partly in the nature of the fossil record and partly in the act of classification.

The amount of fossil material from australopiths is not large, given the long history of the genus. Most of that evidence is highly fragmentary, consisting of bits of broken bone. Scientists are finding DNA increasingly useful for establishing relationships among modern species, but there is no way to obtain DNA from fossils millions of years old. Piecing together the story of evolution and interrelationships among the australopiths and other possible hominins is like trying to read a book that has most of its pages missing, and may be lacking some letters of the alphabet as well.

Deciding where the boundaries lie between species can be tricky even for biologists who study living creatures. Within each species, individuals show a wide range of morphologies, or physical forms. Take humans, for example. A future scientist looking at the skeletons of everyone in your town would see a lot of variations: broad shoulders and narrow ones, long legs and short ones, large hands and small ones. People's skulls can even have different shapes and thicknesses of bone. With the population of a whole town to study, the scientists would know that human beings can display a broad spectrum of skeletal differences, even though we are all one species. But imagine that the future scientist has just three pieces of evidence: part of a thighbone from a very short adult, a teenager's jawbone, and some finger bones from an elderly person. The scientist might not find it immediately obvious that all of these specimens came from the same species.

Some biologists are splitters and some are lumpers. A splitter tends to focus on the differences between organisms, seeing these differences as signs that the organisms belong to separate species. A lumper tends to focus on the things organisms have in common, lumping individuals into the same species on the basis of shared features. For these reasons the classification of hominin fossils is an ongoing debate, and the number of australopith species varies somewhat from one paleoanthropologist to another.

A. anamensis

The oldest generally recognized species of australopith is A. anamensis. A few fossils of this species were found at two sites near Kenya's Lake Turkana in the late 1960s. Paleontologists knew that the fossils belonged to the hominid family but were unable to classify them more precisely. At that time Australopithecus was known only from South Africa. Later, after the discovery of Lucy, paleoanthropologists decided that the Lake Turkana finds were

Australopithecus anamensis *from East Africa is one of the lesser-known hominins. Some scientists question whether it is truly an australopith.*

another new species of australopith. The fossils from Lake Turkana received the scientific name *A. anamensis.*

No complete *Australopithecus anamensis* skull has been found, but scientists do have a lower and an upper jawbone. From these they can tell that the teeth were arranged like an ape's, in two straight lines along the sides of the mouth and a shorter straight line across the front, rather than in a curving arc like human teeth. This tooth arrangement would have given *A. anamensis* an "orangutan-like snout."[38]

A. anamensis has been dated to between 4.2 and 3.8 million years ago, but it is poorly known because so few fossils are available. Some paleoanthropologists think that the species does not belong with the australopiths. They argue that it should be reassigned to *Ardipithecus* or another genus. In 2006 Tim White found fossils in the Afar region of Ethiopia that resemble *A. anamensis*. In White's view, the species that has been called *A. anamensis* belongs on an evolutionary line between *Ardipithecus* and *A. afarensis*.[39]

A. afarensis

Lucy and Selam's species, *A. afarensis*, is known from fossils found in Ethiopia and Tanzania. The dating of these fossils ranges from 4 million to 2.8 million years ago. *A. afarensis* is much better known than *A. anamensis* because scientists have recovered so many fossils. Compared with the dental arrangement of *A. anamensis*, Lucy's species shows the beginning of a smooth curve in the tooth row.

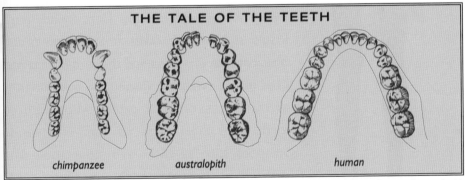

THE TALE OF THE TEETH

chimpanzee   australopith   human

In teeth as in some other features, australopiths fall midway between apes and humans. A row of australopith teeth is more curved than that of a chimpanzee, but less curved than that of a human.

A. africanus

In the years since Raymond Dart found the Taung child fossils in a box, researchers have recovered hundreds of *A. africanus* fossils from the two South African sites where Dart and Robert Broom excavated, Makapansgat and Sterkfontein. Most of these fossils are about 2.4 or 2.5 million years old, although some have been dated to 3.5 million years ago. The fossils show that *A. africanus*, like the other australopiths, was a mixture of humanlike and apelike features. Its teeth were smaller relative to body size than those of apes,

A. africanus was mostly vegetarian.

though larger than those of humans. Its hands were humanlike, too, although they were larger in proportion to the body than human hands.

A. africanus has been found only in South Africa. Scientists think that this species evolved among the somewhat earlier australopiths further north and then migrated south. One theory among paleoanthropologists is that both *A. afarensis* and *A. africanus* descended from *A. anamensis*.

South Africa's extensive limestone deposits are the reason for the lime mining that brought the Taung fossils to Raymond Dart's attention. When Robert Broom and Dart found more fossils in limestone caves at Sterkfontein and Makapansgat, Dart decided that *A. africanus* had lived in the caves. He viewed the australopiths as carnivores, or meat eaters, who ventured forth from their caves to hunt with crude weapons such as sticks and stone tools. The prey they brought back to their caves accounted for the many animal bones that Dart found there, mixed up with the australopith bones.

Scientists now have a different view of *A. africanus*, based on detailed studies of the caves and the bones. The australopiths were not cave dwellers. Instead, they could have been carried to the caves as the prey of large carnivores such as saber-toothed cats and hunting hyenas. These carnivores' own remains have been found in the caves.[40] The carnivores may have used the caves as dens, or they may have eaten their prey in trees that overhung the openings of underground caves, as leopards are known to do today, allowing the bones to fall into the pits. It is also possible that australopiths and other animals simply fell into underground cavities and were trapped there. Erosion later turned these pits into open caves.

Based on tooth structure and markings, scientists think that A. africanus ate a broad range of foods: soft fruits when they were available, as well as harder fruits, nuts, and seeds. One study of minerals in the teeth and bones suggested that the diet of these australopiths included grass seed or animals that had eaten grass.[41] Like modern chimpanzees, australopiths may have eaten mostly plant foods but also consumed insects and grubs, eggs, and small animals when they could get them. They could also have scavenged meat from carcasses—a possibility suggested by the next species of australopith.

A. garhi

Scientists know very little about Australopithecus garhi. The only evidence for this species comes from some 2.5-million-year-old bones found during the 1990s at several sites in Ethiopia's Afar triangle. The fossils consist of jaws, teeth, skull fragments, and some pieces of leg and arm bones. The limb bones and skull pieces were found in different places, so they may not belong to the same species. If they do, then A. garhi had longer legs than the other australopiths. Paleoanthropologists do not yet know whether A. garhi is related to, or descended from, the other australopith species.

What excited paleoanthropologists about A. garhi was not the australopith's fossils but something else from the layer of sediment in which the fossils were found: antelope bones that appear to have been smashed open with rocks. The antelope bones also show cut marks, signs that are left when meat is cut off the bone with a tool such as a knife or sharp-edged stone. In paleoanthropology, cut marks are signs of tool use and meat eating. Someone used sharp-edged stones to remove meat from the antelope bones and then smashed the bones with rocks to get at the nutritious bone marrow inside—probably after scavenging the carcass, not killing the ante-lope. The marks on these bones are among the oldest known signs of tool use. Did *A. garhi* make them?

Scientists cannot be sure. Other kinds of hominins, members of the genus *Homo*, began appearing in the Afar triangle around *A. garhi*'s time, when the oldest known stone tools also appeared. The traditional view was that *Homo* made and used the tools. But although there is no unmistakable evidence that australopiths were tool users, modern chimpanzees—whose brains are about the same size as australopiths' brains—are tool users. Chimpanzees are known to "fish" for termites with twigs and to smash nuts with rocks. The question of whether *A. garhi* used a sharp rock to cut a few steaks from an ancient antelope remains open.

Chimpanzees use stones as tools. Did ancient australopiths do so, too?

A. bahrelghazali

One of the members of the expedition that found the very old *Sahelanthropus* fossil in Chad in 2001 was French paleontologist Michel Brunet, who had already made hominin history. In 1993 Brunet found some teeth and part of a jawbone in the Bahr el Ghazal, the dried-up watercourse of an ancient river in Chad. Brunet and his colleagues dated the fossils to between 3 and 3.5 million years ago. They identified them as a new species of australopith that they named *Australopithecus bahrelghazali.* Some paleoanthropologists, however, believe that the fossils may belong to A. *afarensis,* or that the amount of fossil material from the Bahr el Ghazal is too small to identify for certain. Whatever its final classification may be, Brunet's find was the first sign that early hominins had lived outside the Great Rift area of eastern and southern Africa.

Paranthropus

Remember *Plesianthropus,* Robert Broom's fossil skull that came to be known as Mrs. Ples? Scientists later decided that this hominin belonged to the Taung child's species, *Australopithecus africanus,* and they dropped the genus name *Plesianthropus.* Broom's other major find was the thick-boned, big-jawed skull he named *Paranthropus robustus.* Its relationship to the australopiths is a matter of much scientific debate.

In the late twentieth century, with australopith discoveries and studies booming, most paleoanthropologists felt that P. *robustus* really belonged to the genus *Australopithecus.* They renamed it A. *robustus* and decided that there were two basic forms of australopiths: gracile (slender) and robust (heavily built).

Later, when fossils similar to A. *robustus* began turning up in East Africa, many experts felt that they represented new species of robust australopiths. Many of them still feel that way. In recent years, however, some paleoanthropologists have concluded that the robust australopiths from both South and East Africa are simply too different from the other australopiths to belong to the same genus. They have restored the old *Paranthropus* genus to include these hominins.

While paleoanthropologists differ on how to classify the robust hominins, some things about these species are clear. They arrived on the scene later than most of the australopiths, living at the same time as the early species of *Homo*. For this reason the story of *Paranthropus* (or the robust australopiths) belongs with the beginnings of *Homo* in the next phase of human evolution, described in the second volume of this series, *First Humans.*

Kenyanthropus or *Australopithecus*?

A paleoanthropological expedition found a fragment of an upper jaw and part of a broken skull near Lake Turkana in Kenya in the late 1990s. The skull pieces were in poor condition and badly worn, possibly from erosion or abrasion by river rocks at some point in their history. Because the fossils were found between layers of volcanic ash that can be dated, they are known to be about 3.3 to 3.5 million years old.[42] The skull is about as old as Lucy, in other words, but it does not look like Lucy. Its cheekbones jut forward, giving it a flatter face than the other australopiths, whose jaws stick out farther than their cheekbones.

The find was named *Kenyanthropus platyops*, "flat-faced man from Kenya," although some paleontologists think it belongs in the genus *Australopithecus*. Tim White, for example, feels that the skull is too damaged to be the basis for a new genus. In his view, *Kenyanthropus* could be a variety of *A. afarensis*.[43] Another possibility is that *Kenyanthropus* may not even belong to the human lineage. Without post-cranial remains such as legs and feet, experts cannot be positive that *Kenyanthropus* is not part of the ape lineage. More and better fossils are needed before this flat-faced find can be placed in its true relationship to human evolution.

Were the australopiths human ancestors? Most paleoanthropologists think so, although they do not know which species of *Australopithecus* gave rise to the genus *Homo*. *A. afarensis* and *A. africanus* are possibilities, but it is also possible that intermediate species, or even whole new genera of ancestors, wait to be excavated from the African fossil grounds. But scientists must form the best theories they can from the information at hand, and most now see australopiths perched securely on the human family tree.

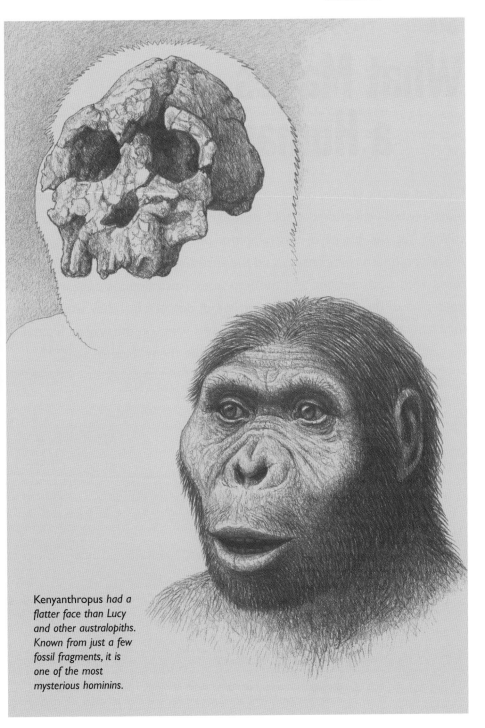

Kenyanthropus *had a flatter face than Lucy and other australopiths. Known from just a few fossil fragments, it is one of the most mysterious hominins.*

SIX
What Makes a Human?

If recent genetic studies of human and chimpanzee DNA are right, australopiths existed well after the split between the lines leading to humans and chimps. Yet the brains of australopiths, on average, were no larger than those of modern chimpanzees, and the australopiths shared many other features with both ancient and modern apes. Australopiths appear to have been part of the hominin lineage, or line of descent, but they were not yet fully human. The chief clue that australopiths were on the way to becoming human lies in a phrase often used to describe them: "bipedal apes."[44]

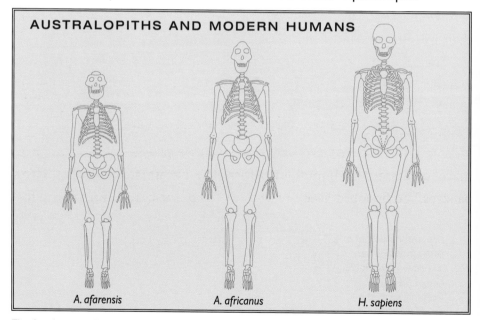

AUSTRALOPITHS AND MODERN HUMANS

A. afarensis   A. africanus   H. sapiens

The feet, legs, and hips of australopiths are very similar to those of modern humans. Australopiths' arms are proportionally longer, however, their braincases are much smaller, and their rib cages are shaped like those of apes. Human features did not all appear at the same time

Before the discovery of australopiths and other very early hominids, people thought that the defining characteristics of "humanness"—having big brains, walking upright, using tools—had all appeared at about the same time in human evolution. We now know that human ancestors walked upright long before they developed big brains. And while the australopiths may have used tools, at least toward the end of their span in existence, the evidence is scanty. Researchers regard bipedalism as the first major shift in the transition from ape to human.

Why Walk Upright?

Ancestral primates spent most of their time in trees—most primates still do—but some of them came to the ground. Among the living primates, baboons and chimpanzees spend a lot of time on the ground, and mountain gorillas spend almost all of their time there. These ground-living primates are quadrupeds, walking on all four legs. Baboons walk with four flat feet, while gorillas and chimps walk on flat rear feet and the knuckles of their front feet.

The ancestors of humans were the only ground-living primates that evolved into full-time bipeds. At one time evolutionary scientists thought that the reason some apes became bipeds was climate change. This idea came to be called the savanna hypothesis. It said that the switch to upright walking took place when savanna grasslands replaced dense forest over much of eastern and southern Africa. The ancestors of gorillas, chimpanzees, and bonobos lived in places that kept their thick, year-round forest cover, so they did not have to change their method of locomotion, or moving about. The ancestors of humans, however, lived in the areas that were most affected by the change in climate and ecology. They had to adapt to life on the savanna.

Like the other hominids, these human ancestors still spent a high percentage of their time in trees, gathering fruit and nuts, but they had to travel over greater and greater distances to get from one tree to the next. Walking upright on these treks let them see over the tall grass so that they could be alert for predators. An upright stance also reduced the amount of body surface that was directly exposed to the hot sun. Physical variations made it easier for some hominids to stand and walk upright than others, giving those hominids a survival edge. Over time those favorable changes spread through the population. The pelvis, hips, legs, feet, and spine of these partic-ular hominids evolved to support upright walking, and bipeds were born.

Research over the past few decades has shown that the savanna hypoth-esis does not fit the facts. The first members of the hominid family that show clear evidence of bipedalism were the australopiths, and they did not live on the savanna. Scientists know this because they have made close examinations of the plant and animal fossils found in the same regions and layers as australopith fossils. By identifying the assemblages of plants and ani-mals in the environments of early hominids, biologists have learned about the kinds of growing conditions, food resources, and habitat that were needed to support those assemblages.

Early hominids such as *Orrorin* and *Ardipithecus*, as well as the australo-piths, lived in settings that were neither tropical forest nor open savanna. Their typical habitat was subtropical forest or open woodland, with sea-sonal patterns of weather, rainfall, and vegetation. These tree-covered areas were sunnier and less dense than tropical or even subtropical forests today, with some open ground.

During the span of australopith evolution, woodlands in East and South Africa became more open and drier, but the fossil evidence shows that aus-tralopiths continued to live in a diverse environment made up of dry forests, wooded grasslands, and lakes or marshes. Today the Afar region of Ethiopia is treeless and arid, for example, but in Lucy's lifetime, some 3.2 mil-lion years ago, it was a place of woodlands and wetlands. "Hominids did not live in full-blown savannas," says science writer Carl Zimmer, "until about two million years ago."[45] By that time hominids were fully bipedal. If the savanna did not make them stand up, what did?

How Australopiths Lived and Moved

Now that scientists know that bipeds evolved in the forest, they are examining new ideas about how bipedalism got started. One idea is that the ancestor of gorillas, chimpanzees, and humans spent time both in trees and on the ground. When it was in the trees, this ancestor sometimes stood erect on branches to reach fruit on higher branches. When it was on the ground, it walked on all four feet, but it sometimes stood up to pick fruit that was hanging overhead. This standing behavior eventually developed into bipedalism in one group of descendants, the human lineage.

Or, suggests Robin Crompton of the University of Liverpool in England, walking started in trees. Crompton, who has studied locomotion in many species, points out that orangutans walk through trees with their bodies erect, striding along branches and holding other branches or vines with their hands. Crompton thinks that bipedalism may have its origins very far back in the human family tree, in the ancestor that humans share with all of the great apes, including orangutans. This hominid ancestor would have lived 12 to 15 million years ago, before the orangutans split off from the other apes. In this theory, hominids' skeletons and muscles started adapting to upright movement while the hominids were still largely arboreal. Two lines descended from the "tree-walking" ancestor. The orangutan line remained in the trees, but the line leading to gorillas, chimpanzees, and humans came down to the ground, at least part-time. The gorilla and chimpanzee lineages evolved into knuckle-walkers. The ancestors of humans became bipeds.

How, when, and why human ancestors became bipeds remains open to question. Another question concerns just how bipedal our ancestors really were. The australopiths were smaller than modern gorillas and chimpanzees, which might have made them nimble climbers. Most paleoanthropologists agree that they were partly arboreal, gathering food and possibly sleeping in trees. (The fossil record has not yielded evidence about family or social life, but australopiths probably foraged for food, slept, and moved about in troops, bands, or family groups as most modern apes do.)

Some researchers have questioned whether australopiths were full-time bipeds when they were on the ground. The joints, bones, and limb proportions of Australopithecus africanus, for example, have been interpreted in various ways. One view is that A. africanus was "a four-legged ground moving early hominid that still retained the ability to climb trees and spent considerable time standing on two legs and in erect trunk postures during feeding."[46] In other words, the Taung child's species was a quadruped that climbed trees and often stood up to eat. Others think that A. africanus "regularly walked upright, sharing this unique mode of locomotion with humans."[47]

The majority view is that the australopiths walked upright. Lucy and the other known australopiths were "definitely bipedal," say paleoanthropologists Chris Stringer and Peter Andrews.[48] Studies at Arizona State University and the University of Liverpool supported this position. Researchers created three-dimensional computer models of Lucy's skeleton and determined that her most efficient form of locomotion would have been upright walking. She would not have walked like a modern human, however. Her top speed was probably about a mile an hour, and her hips swung forward with each step.[49]

Human ancestors did not become bipedal all at once, in a single bold stroke of evolution. The transition to human-style bipedalism took time, and it may have affected other aspects of hominin life. With chimplike hands but humanlike feet, for example, young australopiths like the Dikika child could grasp their mothers' hair with their hands but not with hands and feet both, as chimpanzee infants do. Australopith mothers would have had to do more to support their young as they carried them. Having their hands full in this way may have increased the mothers' dependence on others in the group, strengthening bonds with their relatives or mates.

Bipedalism may be linked to another key human feature: language. Dean Falk, a specialist in the evolution of primate and human brains, points out that once infants could no longer cling tightly to their mothers with four

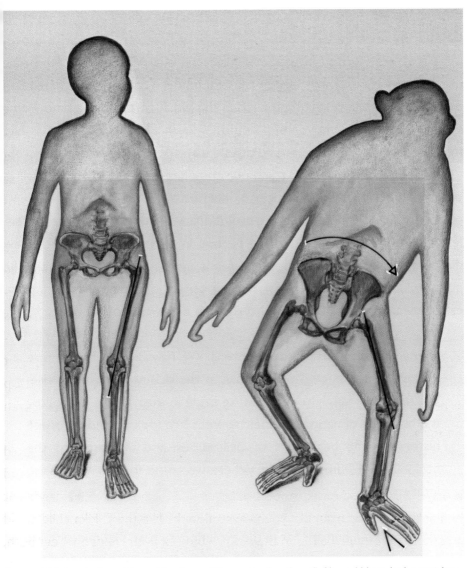

An ape (right) rocks from side to side when walking on two legs. Lucy (left) would have had a straighter stride but would have moved a hip forward with each step, unlike a modern human.

limbs, mothers probably set their young down more often while they moved about gathering food. If mothers made sounds to reassure their young that they were nearby, such communications might have become the foundation on which spoken language developed.[50]

{ 93 }

"Where *We* Come From"

One of the most important discoveries about human origins is the knowledge that our current situation is highly unusual. We are now the only hominin species on Earth, but for most of hominin history there have been multiple species in our lineage, sharing the world at the same time. *Homo sapiens* is the only survivor of a branching bush of evolution that has had many parallel lines, offshoots, and dead ends.

Will we ever be able to trace our complete human lineage far back in time to the last common ancestor shared by both humans and chimpanzees? Or even to sort out the evolutionary relationships among the different kinds of australopiths? Maybe not in every detail, yet each new discovery in a fossil field or a genetics lab is another piece of the puzzle. The quest will certainly continue, for our curiosity about our origins is a powerful driving force. As Donald Johanson, the discoverer of Lucy, says:

Human fossils work a special magic. We have always been more interested in our own origins than in the origins of anything else. We trace our family roots and take pride in their length. We follow the histories of nations to their sources. We look behind recorded history to the beginnings of civilizations, and ultimately to the beginnings of humanity itself. Where *we* come from is where the interest lies.[51]

What makes a human? Far in the evolutionary past, that question is hard to answer. As we move closer to ourselves, "humanness" becomes easier to recognize. The australopiths brought bipedalism into the human lineage. As we will discover in book two of this series, the next group of hominin species to arise would, in time, become recognizably human.

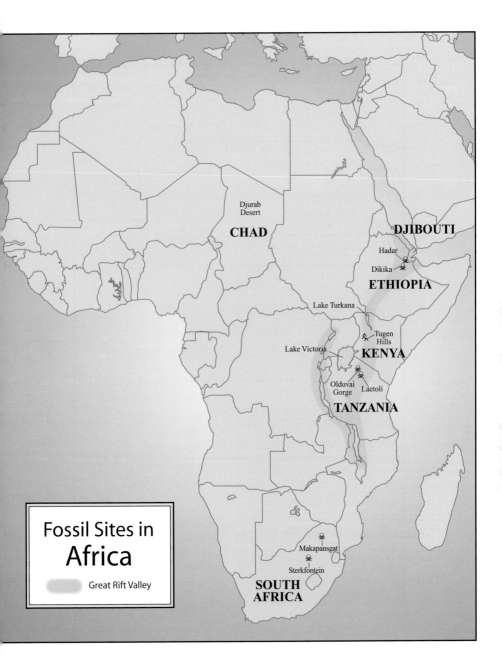

Fossil Sites in
Africa

Great Rift Valley

Geological Time Periods

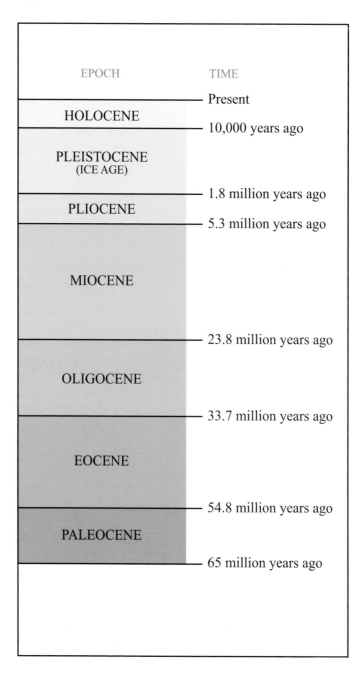

EPOCH	TIME
	Present
HOLOCENE	
	10,000 years ago
PLEISTOCENE (ICE AGE)	
	1.8 million years ago
PLIOCENE	
	5.3 million years ago
MIOCENE	
	23.8 million years ago
OLIGOCENE	
	33.7 million years ago
EOCENE	
	54.8 million years ago
PALEOCENE	
	65 million years ago

Time Line of Human Evolution

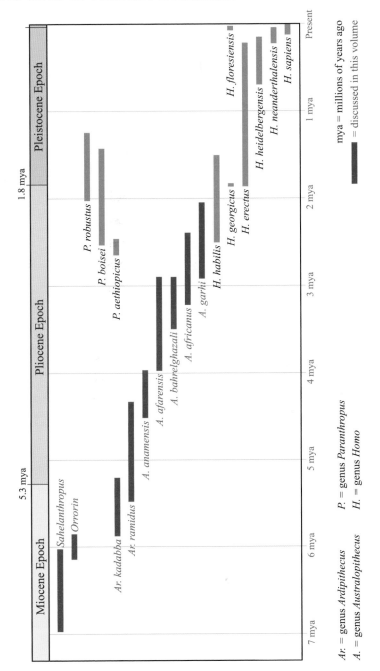

Miocene Epoch

Pliocene Epoch

Pleistocene Epoch

5.3 mya

1.8 mya

7 mya 6 mya 5 mya 4 mya 3 mya 2 mya 1 mya Present

Sahelanthropus
Orrorin

Ar. kadabba
Ar. ramidus

A. anamensis
A. afarensis
A. bahrelghazali
A. africanus
A. garhi

P. robustus
P. boisei
P. aethiopicus

H. habilis
H. georgicus
H. erectus
H. heidelbergensis
H. neanderthalensis
H. floresiensis
H. sapiens

mya = millions of years ago
■ = discussed in this volume

Ar. = genus *Ardipithecus*
A. = genus *Australopithecus*

P. = genus *Paranthropus*
H. = genus *Homo*

Modern Discoveries about Our Earliest Ancestors

1856 Bones of an ancient human found in the Neander Valley, Germany.

1859 Charles Darwin publishes *On the Origin of Species*, introducing evolution.

1863 Thomas Henry Huxley publishes *Evidence as to Man's Place in Nature*.

1871 Darwin publishes *The Descent of Man.*

1921 Human fossils first found in Africa, at Broken Hill mine.

Australopithecus africanus

1924 Raymond Dart receives the Taung child fossil and is first to identify *Australopithecus*.

1947 Robert Broom finds the first *Paranthropus* fossils in South Africa.

1967 Studies of immune properties of proteins show human and chimpanzee ancestors split 5 million years ago.

1973 Donald Johanson finds a knee joint in Ethiopia that proves bipedalism existed 3 million years ago.

1974 Johanson and others discover 40 percent of Lucy, *Australopithecus afarensis*; fossil tooth of *Orrorin tugenensis* found in Kenya.

1976–1979 Mary Leakey excavates fossilized hominin footprints at Laetoli, Tanzania.

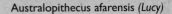

Australopithecus afarensis *(Lucy)*

1990s Fossils of *Australopithecus garhi* found in Ethiopia, near signs of tool use.

1992 Gen Suwa finds *Ardipithecus* tooth in Ethiopia.

2000 Tilahun Gebreselassie finds an infant *Australopithecus afarensis* at Dikika, Ethiopia.

2001 *Sahelanthropus*, between 6 and 7 million years old, found in Chad.

2006 Genomic research suggests ancestors of humans and chimpanzees interbred as they diverged between 6.3 and 5.4 million years ago.

2008 The Laetoli trackway's protective cover reported to be breaking down.

Glossary

adapt To change or develop in ways that aid survival in the environment.

anatomy The physical structure of an organism.

arboreal Living primarily in trees.

australopith Member of the genus *Australopithecus* or *Paranthropus*, several species of small-brained, bipedal human ancestors known from African fossils; also called australopithecine.

bipedal Walking upright on two legs.

DNA Deoxyribonucleic acid, the substance that contains the genetic code or blueprint for each individual and is found inside the cells of living things.

evolution The pattern of change in life forms over time, as new species, or types of plants and animals, develop from old ones.

extinct No longer existing; died out.

foramen magnum The hole in a skull through which the spinal cord passes from the brain to the backbone.

fossil Organic material such as bone or plant matter that has mineralized, or turned to stone, over time.

genetic Having to do with genes, material made of DNA inside the cells of living organisms. Genes carry information about inherited characteristics from parents to offspring and determine the form of each organism.

genomics The study and comparison of genomes, which are the complete genetic codes or blueprints for each species.

hominid Member of the family Hominidae, which includes living and extinct orangutans, gorillas, chimpanzees, bonobos, and humans; term was formerly used for humans and their ancestors.

hominin Member of the tribe Hominini, which includes living and extinct species in the evolutionary line that split from apes and produced humans; formerly called hominids.

hominine Member of the subfamily Homininae, which includes living and extinct humans, chimpanzees, and bonobos.

hominoid Member of the superfamily Hominoidea, which includes all living and extinct apes and humans.

mammal Warm-blooded animal that gives birth to live young and nurses the young with milk from mammary glands.

morphology Physical form.

paleoanthropology The study of ancient human life and human origins, mainly through fossils and other physical remains.

paleontology The study of ancient life, mainly through fossils.

primate Member of the order of mammals that includes humans, apes, monkeys, lemurs, and other small animals.

quadrupedal Walking on four legs.

species Group of organisms that share a genome and are reproductively isolated from other organisms.

taxonomy The scientific system for classifying living things, grouping them in categories according to similarities and differences, and naming them.

terrestrial Living primarily on the ground.

Further Information

Books

Anderson, Dale. *How Do We Know the Nature of Human Origins: Great Scientific Questions and the Scientists Who Answered Them.* New York: Rosen Publishing Group, 2004.

Fleisher, Paul. *Evolution: Great Ideas of Science.* Minneapolis, MN: Lerner Publishing, 2005.

Gamlin, Linda. *Eyewitness: Evolution.* New York: DK Publishing, 2000.

Gardner, Robert. *Human Evolution.* New York: Franklin Watts, 1999.

Lewin, Roger. *Human Evolution: An Illustrated Introduction.* 5th edition. Hoboken, NJ: Wiley-Blackwell, 2004.

Lockwood, Charles. *The Human Story: Where We Come From & How We Evolved.* New York: Sterling, 2008.

McKie, Robin. *Ape/Man: Adventures in Human Evolution.* London and New York: BBC Books, 2000.

Sloan, Christopher. *The Human Story: Our Evolution from Prehistoric Ancestors to Today.* Washington, DC: National Geographic, 2004.

Stefoff, Rebecca. *The Primate Order.* New York: Marshall Cavendish Benchmark, 2006.

Walker, Denise. *Inheritance and Evolution.* North Mankato, MN: Smart Apple Media, 2006.

Wood, Bernard. *Human Evolution: A Very Short Introduction.* New York: Oxford University Press, 2006.

Web Sites

http://www.amnh.org/exhibitions/permanent/humanorigins/

The companion site to the new Hall of Human Origins in New York City's American Museum of Natural History offers information about human evolution and video interviews with scientists Ian Tattersall and Rob DeSalle, curators of the exhibit.

http://www.pbs.org/wgbh/evolution/library/07/index.html

The PBS online *Evolution Library* links to pages on a number of topics, including human evolution. On the "Finding Lucy" page, Donald Johanson describes finding the remains of the famous early hominin. Other pages feature the Laetoli trackway and scientific debates about the switch from four legs to two.

http://anthropology.si.edu/humanorigins/faq/encarta/encarta.htm

The Smithsonian Institution's *Human Origins Program* is an online guide to resources that explain dozens of topics in paleoanthropology and human evolution, from primate origins to the cultural and social evolution of modern humans.

http://evolution.berkeley.edu/evolibrary/home.php

The University of California at Berkeley's *Understanding Evolution* site provides excellent explanations of many topics in general evolutionary biology and includes an archive of articles about human evolution, geared for general audiences.

http://www.talkorigins.org/faqs/homs/

The *Talk Origins Archive* links to dozens of articles on the topic of human evolution. The site also contains information about the creationist position against evolution.

http://www.bbc.co.uk/sn/prehistoric_life/human/

The Science and Nature division of the British Broadcasting Corporation (BBC) maintains this site on *Human Beginnings*. A section called "Evolution of Man" is devoted to Lucy and other early hominins.

http://topics.nytimes.com/top/news/national/series/dnaage/index.html

In a series of articles called the "DNA Age," science writer Amy Harmon describes advances in genetic science and how they are changing our lives as well as helping us learn more about our evolutionary past. Originally published in the *New York Times*, the series won the Pulitzer Prize for explanatory journalism in 2008.

http://www.asu.edu/clas/iho/index.html
http://www.becominghuman.org/

The Institute of Human Origins (IHO) at Arizona State University maintains these two Web sites. *Becoming Human* includes an interactive video documentary, while the main IHO site features a page on "Lucy's Story."

http://www.survivingexhibit.org/
Surviving: The Body of Evidence is the online companion to an exhibit about human origins at the University of Pennsylvania Museum of Archaeology and Anthropology. Among other features, the site has biographies of discoverers such as Charles Darwin and Mary Leakey.

http://www.archaeologyinfo.com/evolution.htm
The "Human Ancestry" page of this archaeology-focused site has a virtual Hall of Skulls, with photos and descriptions of important hominid and hominin fossil finds.

http://www.nature.com/nature/focus/hominiddevelopment/
The science journal *Nature* has gathered articles and information about the Dikika Baby on this Web site, which includes a video interview with the fossil's discoverer.

http://www.bbc.co.uk/sn/prehistoric_life/tv_radio/wwcavemen/
Walking with Cavemen, a companion site to a 2003 BBC television series, includes information about human ancestors as well as an interactive "Caveman Challenge."

Selected Bibliography
The author found these works especially helpful when researching this book.

DeSalle, Rob, and Ian Tattersall. *Human Origins: What Bones and Genomes Tell Us About Ourselves.* College Station, TX: Texas A&M University Press, 2008.

Sawyer, G. J., and Viktor Deak, editors. *The Last Human: A Guide to Twenty-Two Species of Extinct Humans.* New Haven, CT: Yale University Press, 2007.

Stringer, Chris, and Peter Andrews. *The Complete World of Human Evolution.* New York: Thames & Hudson, 2005.

Zimmer, Carl. *Smithsonian Intimate Guide to Human Origins.* New York: Madison Press, 2005.

Notes

Introduction
1 Quoted in Donald Johanson and Maitland Edey, *Lucy: The Beginnings of Humankind*, New York: Warner Books, 1981, p. 41.
2 Richard Milner, *Encyclopedia of Evolution*, New York: Henry Holt, 1990, p. 106.
3 Charles Darwin, *On the Origin of Species*, New York: Avenel, 1979, reprinted from first edition of 1859, p. 435.
4 Darwin, *Origin*, p. 455.
5 Darwin, *Origin*, p. 458.
6 Alexander Pope, *Essay on Man*, Epistle II, line 2, 1733–1734.
7 Rob DeSalle and Ian Tattersall, *Human Origins: What Bones and Genomes Tell Us About Ourselves*, College Station, TX: Texas A&M University Press, 2008, p. 21.

Chapter One
8 Quoted in Richard Milner, *Encyclopedia of Evolution*, New York: Henry Holt, 1990, p. 229.
9 Quoted in Milner, p. 348.
10 Peter Barrett, *Science and Theology Since Copernicus: The Search for Understanding*, London and New York: Clark Publishers, 2004, p. 98.
11 Quoted in Milner, p. 147.

Chapter Two
12 "New Genome Comparison Finds Chimps, Humans Very Similar at the DNA Level,"

NIH News, August 31, 2005, online at
http://www.genome.gov/15515096

13 Roger Lewin, *Human Evolution: An Illustrated Introduction*, New York: Freeman, 1984, p. 13.

Chapter Three

14 "Toumai: The Human Ancestor," Centre National de la Recherche Scientifique, Chad, online at
http://www.cnrs.fr/cw/fr/pres/compress/Toumai/Tounaigb/quiquangb.html

15 G. J. Sawyer and Viktor Deak, editors, *The Last Human: A Guide to Twenty-Two Species of Extinct Humans*, New Haven, CT: Yale University Press, 2007, p. 29.

16 Chris Stringer and Peter Andrews, *The Complete World of Human Evolution*, New York: Thames & Hudson, 2005, p. 116, and Sawyer and Deak, p. 36.

17 Sawyer and Deak, p. 34.

18 Stringer and Andrews, p. 116.

19 Sharon Begley, "Out of Africa, a Missing Link," *Newsweek*, October 3, 1994, p. 56.

20 Roger Lewin, *Human Evolution: An Illustrated Introduction*, New York: Freeman, 1984, p. 19.

21 Feng-Chi Chen and Wen-Hsiung Li, "Genomic Differences between Humans and Other Hominoids and the Effective Population Size of the Common Ancestor of Humans and Chimpanzees," *American Journal of Human Genetics*, February 2001, 68:2, online at
http://www.pubmedcentral.nih.gov/articlerender.fcgi?tool=pubmed&pubmedid=11170892

22 "Evolution's Human and Chimp Twist," BBC News, May 18, 2006, online at
http://news.bbc.co.uk/2/hi/science/nature/4991470.stm

23 Rob DeSalle and Ian Tattersall, *Human Origins: What Bones and Genomes Tell Us About Ourselves*, College Station, TX: Texas A&M University Press, 2008, p. 110.

24 David Brown, "Human Ancestors May Have Interbred with Chimpanzees," *Washington Post*, May 18, 2006, online at
http://www.washingtonpost.com/wp-dyn/content/article/2006/05/17/AR2006051702158_pf.html

Chapter Four

25 Quoted in Richard Milner, *Encyclopedia of Evolution*, New York: Henry Holt, 1990, p. 431.

26 Quoted in Milner, p. 56.

27 Per bizcommunity.com, online at
http://www.biz-community.com/Article.aspx?ai=4673&c=11

28 Quoted in Donald Johanson and Maitland Edey, *Lucy: The Beginnings of Humankind*, New York: Warner Books, 1981, pp. 55–56.

29 Johanson and Edey, p. 98.

30 Johanson and Edey, p. 133.
31 Johanson and Edey, p. 15.
32 Johanson and Edey, p. 18.
33 Owen Lovejoy, PBS Evolution: Library: Laetoli Footprints video, online at http://www.pbs.org/wgbh/evolution/library/07/1/l_071_03.html
34 Quoted in Johanson and Edey, p. 250.
35 G. J. Sawyer and Viktor Deak, editors, *The Last Human: A Guide to Twenty-Two Species of Extinct Humans*, New Haven, CT: Yale University Press, 2007, p. 72.
36 Christopher P. Sloan, "Meet the Dikika Baby," *National Geographic* online, November 2006, at http://ngm.nationalgeographic.com/ngm/0611/feature6/index.html
37 Sloan.

Chapter Five
38 G. J. Sawyer and Viktor Deak, editors, *The Last Human: A Guide to Twenty-Two Species of Extinct Humans*, New Haven, CT: Yale University Press, 2007, p. 50.
39 Sawyer and Deak, p. 54.
40 Sawyer and Deak, p. 101.
41 Charles Lockwood, *The Human Story: Where We Came From and How We Evolved*, New York: Sterling, 2008, p. 40.
42 Sawyer and Deak, p. 59, and Chris Stringer and Peter Andrews, *The Complete World of Human Evolution*, New York: Thames & Hudson, 2005, p. 135.
43 Sawyer and Deak, p. 62.

Chapter Six
44 Carl Zimmer, *Smithsonian Intimate Guide to Human Origins*, New York: Madison Press, 2005, p. 47.
45 Zimmer, p. 52.
46 G. J. Sawyer and Viktor Deak, editors, *The Last Human: A Guide to Twenty-Two Species of Extinct Humans*, New Haven, CT: Yale University Press, 2007, pp. 97–98.
47 Chris Stringer and Peter Andrews, *The Complete World of Human Evolution*, New York: Thames & Hudson, 2005, pp. 124–125.
48 Stringer and Andrews, p. 188.
49 Zimmer, p. 57.
50 Christopher P. Sloan, "Meet the Dikika Baby," *National Geographic* online, November 2006, at http://ngm.nationalgeographic.com/ngm/0611/feature6/index.html
51 Donald Johanson and Maitland Edey, *Lucy: The Beginnings of Humankind*, New York: Warner Books, 1981, p. 68.

Sidebars

52 Chris Stringer and Peter Andrews, *The Complete World of Human Evolution*, New York: Thames & Hudson, 2005, p. 109.

53 Russell L. Ciochon, "The Ape That Was," online at http://www.uiowa.edu/%7Ebioanth/giganto.html

54 Ciochon.

55 Stringer and Andrews, p. 32.

56 Susan Linnee, "First Hominid Footprints Being Covered Over in Tanzania," Connecticut News-Times, September 16, 1996, online at http://www.ntz.info/gen/n00322.html

57 Robin McKie, "Man's Earliest Footsteps May Be Lost Forever," *Observer*, January 13, 2008, online at http://www.guardian.co.uk/science/2008/jan/13/archaeology.oldest.human.tracks.eroding

Index

Page numbers for illustrations are in boldface

About the Author

REBECCA STEFOFF has written many books about natural history and evolution for young adults, including *Chimpanzees* (2004) and *The Primate Order* (2006), both published by Benchmark Books. *The Primate Order* was one of twelve books that she wrote for the FAMILY TREES series, which explored topics in evolutionary science and biology. Stefoff also wrote about evolutionary science in *Charles Darwin and the Evolution Revolution* (1996, Oxford University Press), after which she appeared in the A&E *Biography* program on Darwin and his work. Information about Stefoff and her books for young people is available online at www.rebeccastefoff.com.